A HISTORY OF

PARLIAMENTARY PROCEDURE

Fourth Edition

DARWIN PATNODE

Copyright © 2006 by Darwin Patnode

ISBN 0-7414-3374-5

Author photo by Lee Whitehead.

Published by:

INFI∞ITY
PUBLISHING.COM

1094 New DeHaven Street, Suite 100
West Conshohocken, PA 19428-2713
Info@buybooksontheweb.com
www.buybooksontheweb.com
Toll-free (877) BUY BOOK
Local Phone (610) 941-9999
Fax (610) 941-9959

Printed in the United States of America

Printed on Recycled Paper

Published March 2007

Contents

Preface

to the Fourth Edition

This edition of *A History of Parliamentary Procedure* was produced with the support of a generous grant from Jason and Mary D. Smith of Powell, Ohio, in memory of John N. Dickinson, Ph.D., (1924-86), a dedicated and distinguished teacher of history at Miami University, Oxford, Ohio.

This edition is a substantial rewriting of the third edition, which was published in 1982. In this edition I have expanded the material on the Greek assemblies, the Roman Senate, American colonial procedure, Jefferson's *Manual*, Cushing, Robert, Sturgis, and numerous other subjects. I have also written a new chapter on contemporary international procedure.

I cheerfully acknowledge my debts to various scholars whose works are noted in the pages that follow and also to my deceased friends Lester L. Dahms, Rose C. Dhein, and Richard S. Kain for their original encouragement. I acknowledge the assistance in research of Bruce Hutson and Bernard J. Sussman. I also acknowledge the expert advice of John P. Navins, M.D., regarding Confederate procedure and T. Page Johnson regarding legislative procedure. Special thanks go to Loren Kropat for his expertise on Luther S. Cushing and for access to his database of more than 3,200 parliamentary items and his library of more than 2,000 items as well as Stran L. Trout, compiler of *Parliamentary Procedure Books, A Bibliography*. I also appreciate the advice and help of Margaret Banks, Jonathan M. Jacobs, Jim Lochrie, Eli Mina, Peter Crabtree, Sandy Robertson, Paul McClintock, John Noonan, and many other parliamentarians. Of great value was the encouragement of Barry M. Glazer, M.D.

There are several reasons why I have written on the subject of the history of parliamentary procedure.

The first is simply to show that there *is* a significant body of material relating to the subject, albeit in an uncollected format. There *were* rules of meetings throughout history. They came into existence, they evolved, and some endured through the years. In other words, there truly *is* a history of parliamentary procedure. In fact, a book longer than this one could be written on the subject.

The second reason is to present that corpus of information, not necessarily *in toto* but at least in a readable, manageable manner, without producing an unscholarly book, stressing the main course of the evolution of procedure and certain aspects of it, such as the often-changed motion for the previous question.

The third reason is to suggest how an accurate interpretation of current rules and a full appreciation of them are possible only if one knows their history. I want the reader to be more inclined at the end of the book than at the beginning to see parliamentary procedure in perspective and therefore be more likely than previously to be drawn toward an analytical study of the rules as the products of history, not toward mere speculation as to intent. One's understanding of anything is incomplete until one understands its history.

Most parliamentary rules do not exist just because one person thought they were good or because they spontaneously came forth out of a vacuum; they exist because they came into existence for a reason, they changed for a reason, and some have survived for reasons. Those reasons might have been political or practical. Perhaps some were accidental. Knowing the history of the rules on the casting vote of a presiding officer, the call for the previous or preliminary question, the personal or pecuniary interests that debar one from voting, and the standards of decorum in debate, for example, can influence one's application and interpretation of the rules today.

Thus, although I believe in intense scrutiny of a parliamentary text by itself as an essential prerequisite to a correct understanding of the rules, I also believe that both the meaning and the value of a text may be judged fairly only in the light of history. Only then can the rule be correctly applied to a situation.

My aim, then, must be to cause students and teachers alike to *look* with total accuracy at parliamentary rules, and if I achieve my aim they will be able to echo Matthew Arnold's praise of the ancient Greek, Sophocles:

>"Be his
>My special thanks. . .
>Who saw life steadily and saw it whole."

Chapter 1

Ancient Assemblies and their Procedure

Perhaps the first use of parliamentary procedure occurred at a gathering of cavemen many thousands of years ago. Because writing had not been invented, there were no minutes taken. Presumably there was a proposal, either before or after discussion of a topic, and then agreement, perhaps by vote.

Although some parliamentarians may tell amusing stories about the alleged use of parliamentary procedure in heaven before or after the Battle of the Angels or the use of parliamentary procedure in the Garden of Eden, the Bible does not mention the first event at all and relates the Garden of Eden events in such a way that only the most avid imagination could perceive parliamentary procedure there. In fact, the Bible never uses the word "vote" and rarely uses the word "meeting" in the sense of a gathering of several people to deliberate. Only once does it use the word "presiding," and the context in that instance refers to a gathering of prophets over which Samuel briefly presides in I *Kings* 19:20.

In the ancient Eastern and Egyptian societies, there were undoubtedly some parliamentary deliberations, but the records were never generated or they remain unfound.

In Homer's *Iliad*, the most ancient of literary works in the Western World, there is an instance of a meeting in which the military leader of the Greeks, Agamemnon, and others make a decision in council and then assemble the troops to ratify the decision, datable to a war that occurred about 1250 B.C. This bicameral system--an upper house and a lower house--pervaded ancient Greek legislative history, and it is in ancient Greece that parliamentary procedure may, in its earliest traces, be unearthed, both in private meetings and in public ones.

There is no doubt that there were numerous Greek clubs (that is, permanent, voluntary associations of persons organized for a common end), sacred and secular. Originally these were religious or political entities. Later there were mercantile and trade associations, laborers' groups (including launderers, tanners, gardeners, fishers, bakers, and many more), organizations devoted to the continuation of a native culture among immigrants, and athletic associations, among others. One of the laws of Solon (c. 638-c. 558 B.C.) "gave legal validity to their regulations, unless they were contrary to the laws of the State."[1] Some of these groups existed officially to ensure a decent burial for their members, but they served largely as social groups. Even the labor groups were far more interested in socializing than in advocating economic advantages. Some of the clubhouses of Greek clubs have been excavated.

Often the club meetings would begin with a religious activity, perhaps the source of our modern invocations at meeting openings. There are records from the second half of the second century A.D. that reveal the proceedings, punctuated by the interjections of enthusiastic members, of a general meeting of an urban group, including "a verbatim text of the new statutes of the society unanimously adopted thereat. These deal with the admission and subscription of members, the dates of periodical meetings, the maintenance of order and the penalties imposed for any disorderly behaviour, the religious ceremonies (including a sermon and a dramatic performance by officers and members of the society) which marked the principal meetings, the celebration of any auspicious event in the life of any member, the duties and privileges of the treasurer, and the attendance of members at the funeral of any of their number."[2]

These private assemblies have left us fewer records than the public assemblies have, so let us now turn our attention to the public ones. Ancient Greece was less a nation than a loose confederation of independent city-states, of which the most famous were Athens and Sparta. The customary pattern of governmental organization in the Greek city-states included a king or other ruler function as chief executive, an upper house of advisors to the rule (who was often no more than first among equals), and a lower house, a popular assembly. The upper house was often small, although in some centuries it expanded to as many as five hundred (but it then had an executive committee), and the lower house was invariably large (frequently a few thousand).

In Athens, the lower house was the ecclesia, which means "those summoned." (The term was later adopted by churches to refer to the faithful.) The ecclesia "was nominally the whole body of free Athenian citizens over eighteen years of age; practically it was as many as could be got together, and. . . the maximum attendance did not exceed 5,000. For those legislative acts the validity of which nominally required ratification by the whole people, the number 6,000 was taken to represent the state."[3] The only record of a count, however, "shows 3,461 for and 155 against, total 3,616, a very small proportion of the electorate. There was no quorum required for ordinary business. When a decree was proposed affecting a single individual. . . 6,000 must be present, and in the special case of ostracism [banishment for several years] a six thousand majority was perhaps needed for the decree of banishment to be issued. But it is certain that the average attendance fell far below this figure. During the later years of the Peloponnesian War it was impossible to bring 5,000 citizens together, however important the business. After its close it was so difficult to secure a respectable quorum that payment was introduced for attendance, and the fee was several times increased (perhaps with the decline in value of money) in the course of the fourth century, till it reached a drachma and a half (about an ordinary day's wage) for the ten regular, and a drachma for all exceptional, sittings."[4]

The ecclesia had a regular meeting schedule: it met for a single day ten times per year in regular session, but, over a period of several years, the number of special or extraordinary sessions increased to the point at which they were more extraordinary than regular sessions, with a total of forty meetings per year. Furthermore, the regular sessions became somewhat routine, but the exciting issues of the day were debated in the special sessions. Meetings began in the morning, and members from rural areas had to arise before dawn in order to arrive on time.

Its meeting place in early years was the agora or forum, and the ecclesia was even known as the agora, but in later years it met on the Pnyx, a hill in Athens near the Acropolis, and at other locations, eventually even indoors.

In addition to its quorum, the ecclesia had other rules. For example, it voted by a show of hands, although exact counts were taken when necessary to ascertain the outcome. Occasionally, even a type of ballot was used: two urns were placed respectively for the affirmative and the negative, with chips of pottery deposited, or white and black pebbles were cast into a single urn, or a name might even be written on a chip deposited in an urn. "Voting by ballot seems to have been employed only when the measure was a law applying to an individual or a particular group, or a decree inflicting a severe punishment."[5] Notice of a meeting was required,[6] and there was even a motion equivalent to ordering the previous question (that is, closing debate), particularly by adopting a motion that a proposal be approved without debate.[7] Decision was by majority in most or all cases.[8]

The agenda of the ecclesia, prepared by the upper house, the Council of 500, known as the *Boule*, did not limit the ecclesia so much as one might suspect at first glance. The ecclesia could rearrange items on the agenda and find itself too busy to process certain items. Furthermore, on occasion a motion would be adopted "requiring that at least nine items on the agenda, three under each of the main heads of 'sacred,' 'profane,' and 'foreign affairs,' be considered in a day.[9] Although in theory most legislation originated in the council and was merely confirmed or not confirmed by the ecclesia, in fact the ecclesia had the right to amend a bill as much as necessary, to request the council to submit one, and even to introduce a new bill on the same topic but entirely different.

The presiding officer of the ecclesia was chosen by lot from the council leaders and presided for only one day, thus minimizing any favoritism. The one chosen was not necessarily a good presiding officer. For examples, the philosopher Socrates was chosen and raised a laugh when he did not know quite how to put a question to a vote, according to Plato's *Gorgias*. In another case, Socrates refused to put to vote a question condemning to death several generals, insisting that it was their legal right to have separate votes, according to Xenophon.

If a bill was proposed from the floor of the ecclesia, it could come to a vote only with the consent of the presiding officer and his nine colleagues, but a presiding officer who refused, without sufficient grounds, to allow the ecclesia to vote was liable to prosecution, as he also was if he allowed the ecclesia to vote upon an illegal measure.[10]

The council was divided into ten committees, representing tribes, and the leaders of the committees were present at the ecclesia, in part to keep an eye on their presiding colleague.

During different eras, the rules of debate were different. In early times, any citizen was free to speak to the ecclesia; in later times, all debate was conducted by prominent statesmen, frequently members of the council, with the ecclesia merely listening and then voting. There was a platform for a speaker. Members were ordinarily seated to listen to the debate. The debate might involve simple personal matters, such as bestowing an award on a private citizen, or an important public matter, such as choosing between war and peace. Sometimes experts in a particular subject were invited to speak. There was no time limit on debate. An item incomplete at sundown was postponed to the next day. Interruptions of a speaker were forbidden, but sometimes there would be an outburst. Aeschines, in his speech *Against Timarchus*, lists the following rules: "Speakers in the council or assembly must keep to the subject, must treat each subject separately, must not speak twice on the same subject at the same meeting, must avoid invective, must not interrupt another speaker, must not speak except from the *bema* [platform], must not assault the *epistates* [chairman]."[11]

Certain elections were also conducted in the ecclesia, but the body's decisions on some matters were subject to review by the court system of the time.

It was also in the ecclesia that the first known use of the procedure of reconsideration occurred. In a debate reported by Thucydides concerning the treatment of the residents of the city of Mitylene on the island of Lesbos, there was initially agreement that the whole adult male population of the city would be put to death. After a galley sailed with those orders, voters began to have a change of heart. The authorities were persuaded to put the question to a vote again, and the authorities agreed, sensing that the assembly's members

5

wanted to be able to vote again. In the debate, Cleon, whom Thucydides calls the most violent man at Athens, expressed amazement that anyone would propose to reconsider a decision, for doing so was seemingly illegal or at least contrary to custom, and he questioned the motives of those in favor of reconsideration. He pointed out that "the most alarming feature in the case is the constant change of measures with which we appear to be threatened." Responding to him, Diodotus, who had previously opposed the death penalty, argued persuasively, and the original decision was reversed in time to save the men of Mitylene.[12]

A later debate reported by Thucydides "suggests that the Mitylenian precedent emboldened others to propose reconsidering or reversing decisions of the Assembly. One of the leading Athenian generals of the time, Nicias, was horrified at the folly of the Assembly's decision to send the Athenian fleet to invade Syracuse, a powerful city on the island of Sicily. At a later meeting which was called to consider only the preparations for the fleet, Nicias overtly proposed reconsidering and reversing the decision to sail to Sicily. . . After presenting his case for reversing the decision, Nicias ended his speech with an appeal. . . to put his illegal motion to rescind to a vote."[13] The Athenians in this case did not reverse their decision.

The Council of 500, the upper house of the system, originated as an informal body of elderly and influential advisors to the kind or chief noble. Soon, however, power and nobility outweighed the criterion of age, and what had once been called the council of elders came to be called merely the council. "Where the Council appeared too large--and this could occur in aristocracies at a comparatively low figure--a small ruling committee was often chosen from it, a sort of oligarchy inside an oligarchy; such were the *probouloi* [committee] who seem, as a preparative committee, to have done for the Council what the democratic Council did for the Ecclesia."[14] The people elected an auditor who kept a record of the proceedings of the council. For certain purposes, the council was divided into ten committees, each one being in charge of matters for one tenth of the year. The quorum for such a committee was one third of its membership.

In Sparta, the other famous Greek city-state, the legislative organization was similar: there was a lower house, the apella or assembly, and an upper house, the council. Here, the council was sometimes called the "*gerousia*, or Council of old men, [which] was composed of twenty-eight elders, past the age of sixty, and the two kings. It considered measures to be presented to the apella, or public affairs."[15]

In the election of the members of the *gerousia*, the people assembled and "the candidates for office went through the assembly in an order previously determined by lot. He at whose passing the people raised the loudest cry was held to be elected. The loudness of the cry was judged by men shut up in a house... from which they could hear the cry, but could not see the assembly."[16] Crude tellers were these!

Perhaps the same thought came to one Spartan leader, Sthenlaidas, on a particular occasion: "When Sthenlaidas had thus spoken, he... put the vote to the assembly of the Lacedaemonians [Spartans]. Now in their voting they usually decide by shout and not by ballot, but Sthenlaidas said that he could not distinguish which shout was the louder, and wishing to make the assembly more eager for war by a clear demonstration of their sentiment, he said: 'Whoever of you, Lacedaemonians, thinks that a treaty has been broken and the Athenians are doing wrong, let him rise and go to yonder spot, and whoever thinks otherwise, to the other side.' Then they rose and divided, and those who thought a treaty had been broken were found to be in a large majority."[17] This incident is an early case of the use of a division (a vote in which members stand or move into a certain area).

The rules of the Spartan legislature were similar to those of the Athenian legislature. The council had an executive committee of five members, the board of ephors, which acted by majority vote. The ephors convened both the council and the apella and presided over them. Membership in the apella was limited to Spartans of at least thirty years of age, and the assembly at first met outdoors, perhaps in the marketplace, and then indoors. In early years, debate was open to all; in later years, it was not. Members remained seated to hear debates. Legislation generally originated in the upper house, but historians record several great debates in the apella. Eventually the apella lost its power, and some of its decisions were vetoed by the board of ephors. Shouting, as mentioned above, was the usual method of voting.

Thus, the ancient Greeks provided Western Civilization with the basis of what is now called parliamentary procedure, but they did not do so directly. They were followed by the

Romans, who simultaneously despised the Greeks and yet imitated them.

The Romans, like the Greeks, had their clubs, including trade groups, young people's sports clubs, dining clubs, and veterans associations. The officers of these clubs often had titles corresponding to those of civic officials. The presidents were *magistri* (chiefs, masters) or *curatores* (superintendents, managers). There was an officer in charge of the roll. There were classes of membership.[18]

The legislative organization of the Romans was also similar to that of the Greeks: the upper house was the senate, from the Latin word for old man, and the lower was a popular assembly, which, in theory, represented the entire state and received advice from the senate before making a decision. In reality, however, power gravitated toward the senate. The assembly procedure will be examined later.

Roman Senate procedure can be summarized thus, though there were no written rules: "Sessions were held between dawn and sunset, but were forbidden... during the *Comitia* [the meeting of the lower house]. Only during the Empire were the times of meeting fixed--usually two each month. The meeting had to take place either in Rome... or within a mile of the city, in a place both public and consecrated. The first sitting of the year was held in the temple of Jupiter Capitolinus.

"Sittings were usually held in private, but with opened doors, the tribunes of the plebs [the common people] sitting in the vestibule in the period before their admission to sessions. Each senator spoke from his seat. Freedom of speech was unlimited during the Republic. Augustus imposed a time-limit. First came the report *(relatio)* of the chairman or another magistrate, who submitted it in writing. Each senator was asked *(interrogatio)* his opinion *(sententia)*, according to his rank.... After the debate the different opinions were put to vote by a division *(discessio)*. Sometimes *relatio* was followed by *discessio* without *interrogatio*. Certain resolutions required a quorum. Any resolution... could be vetoed by the tribunes. The urban quaestors [financial officers] kept the records... The publication of official records... ordered by Caesar, was suppressed in part by Augustus. Improvements in shorthand made accurate reports possible."[19]

The previous quotation describes the procedure during regal and republic Rome; during the later imperial age the procedures may have been modified somewhat, and the senate decreased both in membership and in attendance, with mere acclamation often substituted for discussion. In still later years, it may have improved somewhat.

Legislation or main motions had priority on the basis of the originator: motions from consuls came first, those from praetors came second, and those from tribunes came last. This sequence became restrictive only if the consul prematurely dismissed the meeting or if some filibustering senator stalled until the setting sun made termination of the session necessary. Both of those problems actually arose. "In the last few years of the Roman Republic there were recorded a dozen instances of obstruction by talking against time. It is said that the irrepressible Cato carried the practice to triumph in the end. The story is that he was filibustering against an agrarian measure which the presiding consul, Caesar, was very anxious to pass. Caesar ordered the officer we would now call the sergeant-at-arms, to remove him. Cato was removed, but the whole Senate followed him, and no magistrate ever again tried to stop debate."[20]

After debate, the presiding officer put the issue to a vote, but, because many slightly different wordings of the best resolution had been set forth by various senators during the course of debate, the presiding officer could select the wording that he preferred to submit. Although not every senator necessarily spoke in debate, the reader must bear in mind that a senator was always asked the same question, "What do you recommend?" and that the senate at the time of Cicero (106-43 B.C.) had a vote with fifteen on one side and "quite 400" on the other.[21]

"One is sometimes surprised, considering the rigidity of the procedure and the size of the body, at the amount of business that appears to have been transacted at a single meeting of the Senate. Both the rules of procedure and the Roman temperament account for the rapidity of the debate. As regards the former it must be remembered that no motion could be put unless pressed by a magistrate, that there was no distinction between substantive motions and amendments, that alternative proposals, therefore, had not to be submitted in detail to a division, that the carrying of one motion generally swept all *sententiae* on the same subject aside, that motions for adjournment did not take precedence of other motions, and that the business of the house was not interrupted by this modern

9

device for wasting time. We must also remember that a division in the modern sense of the word was rare and that it appears seldom to have been necessary to take the numbers of the members who respectively supported or were adverse to a motion. The estimate of the voting was in fact going on during the debate; it was the custom of the senator, often without rising, to express a few words of assent to a former speech, and it was not unusual to leave one's bench and take up a position near the man whose opinion one supported."[22]

There were still other parliamentary rules governing the senate. For example, it occasionally went into executive session, in which case the doors were closed. Members sat in certain areas reserved for persons of their rank, but within each area a senator could sit where he wished. Members rose when addressing the senate and when the magistrates entered and departed. Usually no quorum was necessary for the transacting of routine business, and attendance was often low. In theory, attendance was compulsory, and the property of senators could be confiscated if they were not present. Before a meeting opened, the presiding officer made an offering to the gods and took the auspices. The legality of business transacted after sundown was questionable. Communications were read at the beginning of the meeting, often concerning the administration of remote regions, sent by those on site. The presiding officer could also summarize a situation. During debate, the practice was to recognize senators, preference going to senators by rank of office previously held, by the word "Speak!" followed by the name of the senator. A low-ranking senator frequently spoke with his feet--that is, he merely walked to the area of a speaker with whom he concurred. A speaker did not necessarily have to make comments strictly germane to the topic at hand. Speeches were not often long, because long speeches were deemed a sign of disrespect for one's colleagues, but they were strong and sometimes even rather personal, interrupted by expressions from senators and from outdoor listeners in some cases. Because the presiding officer had the right to terminate debate when he saw fit and formulate the exact final wording of the proposal, he had a great deal of authority. Senators could, however, require that a complex proposal be divided into parts. Furthermore, once a senator had spoken his approval of a proposal, he could not discuss other competing proposals made later by other senators, although he could change his vote when the vote was finally taken. Abstaining was not a right, and any senator could demand that all senators vote.

Voting was by majority and was conducted in various ways; when a division was necessary, the presiding officer indicated a change of seats by saying, with the gesture of the hand, "You who approve, go here; you who think otherwise, go there." Another kind of division, a division of the question, could be requested, but the presiding officer did not have to grant the request. Secret voting was not allowed, probably because high-ranking senators wanted to see how low-ranking senators voted.

After the vote, the proposal would be reduced to writing, usually by a committee of the presiding officer and proponents. The proposal typically began with a recitation of the facts (this portion is similar to modern "Whereas" clauses), followed by the actions to be taken.

The lower house of the Roman legislature was a popular assembly known as the *comitia*, and its assembly-place was known as the *comitium*. Originally it dealt with adoptions and the installation of priests, but it gradually changed into a different kind of assembly, dealing with legislating, declaring war, and inflicting the death penalty. In any case, it dealt only with business presented to them by presiding officers, and its actions were subject to ratification by the senate. In some cases, the assembly was summoned in groups, and the majority in each group determined the group vote in the assembly. About the third century A.D., the *comitia*, having grown weaker for many decades, faded from existence.

The typical procedure was simple. The people assembled upon notice, although no quorum is known to have existed. The presiding officer opened the meeting with a prayer, and a proposal was read. Various leaders expressed their opinions on it. There was little or no debate among the general populace, and there were no amendments allowed. At the end of the debate, those ineligible to vote were excluded, and the voters were grouped into roped compartments according to rank and tribe. An absent tribe was replaced by persons designated by the presiding officer, and those persons acted as that tribe. Votes were taken by groups, and as soon as enough groups had voted affirmatively to approve a proposal the voting ceased. (Until a reform in the year 241, the nobility or knights always voted first.) During early years the vote was by voice, but toward the end of the second century balloting was employed.[23]

Thereafter, "the state provided little tablets inscribed with abbreviations for 'ut rogas' and 'antiquo' for affirmative and negative votes respectively, and for elections blank tablets on which the names of the candidates could be written."[24] Records of the votes were kept.

But the glory that was Greece and the grandeur that was Rome were not kept.

Chapter 2

Medieval Parliamentary Procedure

Historians often take the year 410 as the fall of Rome and the beginning of the Medieval Age or the Middle Ages, a period between the lost light of Roman civilization and the new light of the Renaissance about a thousand years later. (It was in 410 that invading Huns ravaged the Empire, sacked Rome, and replaced togas with trousers.)

The first half of the Middle Ages is often termed the Dark Ages, and the darkness included more than a disintegration of empire; it included a deterioration in the force of law, a diminishment of knowledge and the arts, and a loss of invaluable records. No longer was civilization headquartered in a senate; indeed, the Roman Forum was used for cattle-grazing. If there was any semblance of civilization, it varied in format from tribe to tribe. Thus, to survey parliamentary procedure in medieval assemblies requires a country-by-country analysis of governing councils.

Although it is not feasible to examine every country's councils in this study, let us begin where we recently ended--in Rome. Each city in Italy was a small kingdom onto itself. Even in mere towns or communes, as they are sometimes called, the field of politics was one of frequent violence. There was agreement on nothing, not even on the method of agreement. Rules of debate and voting were a thing of the past. In all but the smallest bodies, discussion consisted of listening to feuding leaders and voting consisted of shouting one's reaction, even resorting at times to bloodshed.

Gradually, very gradually, there was improvement. For instance, the division and the rising vote returned to usage. Statutes speak of formulas for having an assembly divide into affirmative and negative groups and for having members rise or sit to indicate their votes.

Further development occurred in the conduct of elections within communes. For example, to avoid fraud and violence, elections were often by lot. Under the rules in Brescia, "names of the councillors were placed in a bag and as many lots black and white. . . as there were names were to be provided by the tellers. The tellers, two Minorite friars and two Dominicans, were to mix the names and one by one the names and the lots were to be drawn. Whenever a black lot was drawn, one of the friars records the name of the councilor chosen and the quarter of the city from which he came. When the process was completed the names were read, and the list passed over to the chairman, and the electoral college was thus formed."[25] Note that the election is not only secret and random; it is also indirect: those elected merely proceed to elect someone else.

Also, various other restrictions are known: "In almost all of the cities all persons not directly interested in the drawing of the lots were forbidden to come within three or four yards of the polling-place. In Bologna and Sienna the statutes decreed that the lots marked and unmarked shall be identical in form and substance, so that no one can discern the one from the other. In order to prevent connivance and collusion the electors were required to take strict oaths; with the same object in view, in many cities no two members of the same family could act in the same electoral college, nor could any elector vote for himself or for any member of his family. Most of all, however, the statutes insisted that the election should follow immediately upon the choosing of the electors."[26] Sometimes the electors chosen were limited to three days in which to conduct their election. They might even be sequestered or put on short rations until the election was complete.

Rules governing such a voting process varied even to the point of difference in the vote required for election: "In Genoa the choice seems, as a rule, to be have been a unanimous one, though not necessarily so; in Brescia and in Ivrea a two-

14

thirds vote was necessary to a choice; in Bologna the same proportion, twenty-seven out of forty, or thirteen out of twenty, was preserved; in other cities four-sevenths was the proportion. In all cases more than a mere majority was required to elect a candidate to office."[27]

As voting by ballot spread, further rules developed regarding its details. Rules are known to exist concerning the position of the ballot boxes, the choice of tellers, and instructions to be alert for fraud in the distribution, deposition, and tabulation of ballots. The ballots varied in form: often they were black and white beans, but various other versions are known.

In Italy even more than in other countries one might look to the Catholic Church for guidance, and in medieval times the Church held enormous sway over both private and public life. We should, then, next turn to the Church assemblies. "In the practices of the church, however, one cannot find a consistent method of arriving at decisions. In certain important instances the principle of unanimity was required. The decrees of the Synod of Elvira (305 A.D.) begin with the words, *'Episcopi universi dixerunt* [all the bishops said].' Hefele suggests that the decision reached at the Council of Nicaea (325 A.D.) was not erected into a canon was due to the fact that it was not unanimous. . . . Canon Four of the Council of Nicaea provides that bishops shall be chosen by *all* the bishops of the province."[28] Even secular princes were known to refuse to pay taxes in some instances because the taxes, though approved by the council, had not received *their* vote, and surely a prince did not have to obey a law adopted only by others. In 1179, Pope Alexander III issued a decree requiring a two-thirds vote to elect a pope, and the requirement today is two-thirds plus one. Church rules further provided during the last years of the Middle Ages an elaborate system of security in voting: "The first step in this process was the election of three tellers *(scrutatores)* and three tellers for the tellers *(scrutatores scrutatorum)*. The three tellers then wrote down on tablets the name or names of the candidates whom they wished to vote for, and passed them to their tellers who must keep their places and invited the other cardinals to vote. Each cardinal followed the practice just described, no ballot being revealed till the whole body had voted. Then the tellers opened the ballots and read the names of the cardinals voting and the candidates whom they had voted for. The results were tabulated on tally-sheets, and if some candidate had received a two-thirds vote he was declared elected. If no one had received the required number of votes the process had to be repeated till two-thirds of the college were agreed on one candidate."[29]

Nowadays, it should be noted, there are alternative methods allowed (spontaneous voting by voice and delegation to a committee with final power to decide), the number of tellers has been increased to nine, and certain other details have been added.[30]

Church scholars at one point also maintained that the majority was all that was needed to make a decision, although not necessarily on the election of a pope. These canonists argued that the majority was representative of the whole, while the minority was a mere collection of individuals. (This line of argument still exists: a report of a majority of a committee is a committee report, but the report of other members is merely "minority views.") Thus, when the majority spoke, the whole spoke, and all individuals should assent to the wishes of the whole. Even if a decision was by majority, another rule might define a majority in light of calculations other than numerical. Such factors other than member numbers might include "(1) As to *auctoritas* [authority] all the deciding factors in the external attributes of the individual voters; (2) As to *meritum* [merit] all the advantages and merits of the voters as well as of the candidates; (3) As to *zelus* [zeal] all circumstances allowing an insight into purely spiritual and objective electoral motives or the possible more earthly, sensual, and personal ones."[31]

Now let us turn aside from religious meetings and focus on the pages of Tacitus (c. 55-c. 120), a Roman historian, describing, his *Germania*, a popular assembly of a Teutonic tribe: "It is a foible of their freedom that they do not meet at once when commanded, but a second and a third day is wasted by dilatoriness in assembling; when the mob is pleased to begin, they takes their seats carrying arms. Silence is called for by the priests, who thenceforward have power also to coerce; then a king or chief is listened to, in order of age, birth, glory in war, or eloquence, with the prestige which belongs to their counsel rather than with any prescriptive right to command. If the advice tendered be displeasing, they reject it with groans; if it please them, they clash their spears; the most complimentary expression of assent is this martial approbation."

Several centuries later, Charles IV provided for the election of German kings "according to the majority principle.

In real elections, in the assemblies of rural municipalities, and even more slowly in federative unions, the majority principle began to be introduced. But in the political assemblies the principle of unanimity was raised in opposition to it, and in the rural districts the decisions came to be valid in trade meetings, courts, rural parishes, cities, guilds, and it was declared a general rule in the law books."[32]

The early Teutonic assemblies described by Tacitus also had their influence on what is now known as the world's oldest extant parliament, the Althing of Iceland, founded about 930. The Althing, which meets for only two weeks each year, had various parliamentary rules in its code. The chairman, elected for a term of three years and often re-elected, planned and announced the order of business. Not all members of the Althing were eligible to vote on legislation, but a majority of those eligible to vote on legislation could adopt it. Forty-eight members constituted a quorum, and when a proposal had been adopted all the members of the Althing were then required to give their assent.

In France, the gatherings at the court of the king led to a *parlement*, but its chief concern was judicial, not legislative. Larger gatherings were more representative and thus came closer to being parliaments as understood today. After 1300, two large gatherings were held on a regular basis, one in the northern provinces and one in the southern provinces. The Estates General was first held in Paris in 1302, upon the call of King Philip.

Spain likewise had representative assemblies on an occasional basis during the last centuries of the Middle Ages. "The first recorded appearance of town representatives in the Cortes of Aragon is placed in 1162; the first in Castille in 1169. The general courts of Frederick II in Sicily were framed in 1232; in Germany the cities appear by deputies in the diet of 1255."[33]

The English assemblies, though, are of the greatest interest to us because of their contributions to modern parliamentary procedure. "Early Anglo-Saxon kings, and notably those of Kent and Wessex, were in the habit of pronouncing their laws or 'dooms,' only with the consent of the 'witans,' or assemblies of the great men, lay and clerical, of the state,"[34] according to O'Brien, who quotes documents issued in reference to the subject about 690 and again in 872. Such important gatherings to advise the king "were described as courts *(curiae),* councils *(concilia)* or great councils *(magna concilia),* the latter terms becoming the more usual... The word *parliamentum,* which was doubtless in use in common speech long before, makes it first appearance in 1237 in the *Historia Anglorum* of Matthew Paris, in 1239, in his *Chronica majora,* in 1242 in official documents."[35]

Incidentally, the word *parliamentum* is found in a papal document of Urban II in 1089, again in a history in 1101, and, as *parlement,* in the *Chanson de Roland* in the late 11th century.[36]

From the great councils Parliament was to emerge. "It is, according to Sir Courtenay Ilbert, Clerk of the House of Commons, "a development and expansion of the King's Council, of the Council in which the Norman King [French king--the French William conquering England in 1066] held 'deep speech' with his great men. In the thirteenth century the word Parliament came to be applied to the speech so held on solemn and set occasions. The word signified at first the speech or talk itself, the conference held, not the persons holding it, for 'colloquium' and 'parliamentum' were practically identical. It was, as Professor Maitland says, rather an act than a body of persons. By degrees the term was transferred to the body of persons assembled for conference, just as the word 'conference' itself has a double meaning. The persons assembled were the persons, or the representative of the persons, whom the King found it needful to consult for matters military, judicial, administrative, financial, legislative. . . . They [the proceedings] were partly ceremonial, partly practical. There were formal addresses, and there was doubtless much informal talk about public affairs."[37] The king's financial needs often caused him to seek the cooperation of his councilors. Before the Great Charter or Magna Carta, sealed on June 15, 1215, between King John and the barons, "King John had been forced to rely more and more upon extraordinary revenues for the prosecution of his wars and the indulgence of his other extravagances, and had raised the money principally by means of scutages, a form of regular taxation. The Great Charter. . . forbade the King to levy scutages 'except by common counsel of our kingdom.'"[38] Furthermore, many communities, communes, or commons, as they are sometimes called, had achieved some control over their taxation and other aspects of government. Thus, in 1254, when the king, Henry III, demanded more supplies and the barons or lords were reluctant to interfere in the established workings of the commons, leaders of each of the commons were summoned to what might be considered the first Parliament or at least the first meeting of the House of Commons. The process was repeated and expanded in 1265, and in 1275 King Edward I summoned knights and burgesses to the Parliament to discuss a variety of matters. Thus, gradually, the interests of Parliament grew from such basics as war and peace, taxes, marriage and succession of the king, and legal decisions. In the earliest years of Parliament, a main motion was likely to be a petition, because a chief concern of Parliament was petitioning the king; many decades later, it evolved into a bill, that is, a proposal for a law.

The majority principle, incidentally, which had been the subject of such disagreement during much of the Middle Ages, was enunciated in the Magna Carta, which confers on a group of twenty-five barons a broad extent of powers and then proceeds, "If perchance those twenty-five are present and disagree about anything or if some of them after being summoned are unwilling or unable to be present, that which the majority of those present ordain and command shall be held." This provision was omitted, however, from subsequent reconfirmation of the charter, and the common practice was to resort to the rule only when absolutely necessary.

The Parliament of 1295, summoned by King Edward I, was the most fully representative gathering to its time, might appropriately mark the baptism of Parliament, and is known as the Model Parliament, and in 1339 the House of Commons said that it could not grant aid without consulting those whom it claimed to *represent*.

Chapter 3

Procedure in Parliament, 1340-1832

By 1340, Parliament had solidified into two houses: the upper House of Lords and the lower House of Commons, although the former was not called the House of Lords until the sixteenth century. Until the nineteenth century, procedures in the two houses were similar, except those in regard to debate and methods of maintaining order; also, the presiding officer of the Lords had far less authority in procedure than did the presiding officer of the Commons. Perhaps because the House of Commons increased its power much more than the House of Lords did, especially during the Renaissance, its procedure has been more influential and thus merits more attention in this chapter.

The presiding officer of the House of Commons is called the Speaker (not in the sense of "talker" but in the sense of "spokesman," particularly for the House in communicating to the king), and the first Speaker was Sir Thomas Hungerford (1377). Before him, Sir Peter de la Mere was Speaker in all but name (earlier presiding officers having had various titles, including "parlour"), and the earliest known presiding officer was Peter de Montfort (1258). "The principal function of the Speaker in those early days was to act as the mouthpiece of the Commons and to communicate their resolutions to the King. It was often an unenviable task, and at least nine Speakers are known to have died a violent death, four of them during the turbulent period of the Wars of the Roses. On the other hand, the Speaker frequently turned out to be a King's man, and in the Tudor period he is described by Stubbs as being 'the manager of business on the part of the Crown and probably the nominee either of the King himself or the Chancellor.' He frequently held high office in addition to the Speakership. It has been suggested that the practice of the Speaker in vacating the Chair when the House goes into committee owes its origin to the mistrust once felt by Commons for their presiding officer."[39]

The Speaker has all the powers of a presiding officer, although the following current description was not necessarily applicable in its details during the time of this chapter: "In debate all speeches are addressed to him and he calls upon Members to speak--a choice which is now never disputed. When he rises to preserve order or to give a ruling on a doubtful point he must always be heard in silence and no Member may stand when the Speaker is on his feet. Reflections upon the character or actions of the Speaker may be punished as breaches of privilege. . . . His action cannot be criticized incidentally in debate. . . . Confidence in the impartiality of the Speaker is an indispensable condition. . . . He takes no part in debate either in the House or in committee. He votes only when the voices are equal, and then only in accordance with rules which preclude an expression of opinion upon the merits of a question."[40] In the earliest years of the House, the Speaker would listen to various opinions on a topic and then *compose* and put to vote a proposal of his own devising that would be able to reflect the consensus of the members.

With the powers of the Speaker's office, however, there also come obligations, some of which Speakers of the past have found difficult to uphold. The records of Parliament are studded with references implying displeasure at the conduct of Speakers, and the adoption of rules circumscribing the powers of the Speaker was often the reaction to particular actions taken on behalf of the Crown by Mr. Speaker. An excellent history of the Speakership is to be found as Chapter III of Part VI of Book II of *The Procedure of the House of Commons*,[41] a three-volume work of scholarship by Josef Redlich that covers virtually every other aspect of Parliament's procedure before the twentieth century. Two other valuable works on the rules of Parliament, past and present respectively, are John Hatsell's *Precedents of Proceedings in the House of Commons*[42] and Erskine May's *Treatise on the Law, Privileges, Proceedings and Usage of Parliament*.[43] John Hatsell was an officer of the House of Commons for sixty years, starting in 1760. He compiled several volumes of precedents, publishing the first volume in 1776. Thomas Erskine May was born in 1815 and, at the age of sixteen, appointed assistant librarian of the House of Commons. In 1844, he published his *Treatise*, which has been maintained in subsequent editions to the present. The works differ in that Hatsell deals with lists of precedents, whereas May summarizes the general result of the precedents.

Before 1400, the custom of three readings of bills had become established in the House of Commons. The first reading was for introduction, the second for debate and amendment, and the third for perfection and final approval. For hundreds of years, the entirety of the bill was read aloud by the Clerk (but nowadays printing substitutes for reading, and a committee stage and subsequent debate intervene between second and third readings).

The minutes or journals of the House of Commons were begun on the initiative of the Clerk in 1547 and soon "became established as a source of precedent on matters of procedure. The first recorded instance of such use of the Journal. . . was in 1580 or 1581. The Journal was given official status as a document of the Commons about 1623."[44] In the early days, various notes on the processing of bills were included as well as the final decisions, but this practice was forbidden by resolutions of 1628 and 1640. The journals of the House of Lords began in 1509, somewhat before those of the House of Commons.

During the same century were published the first books on procedure in Parliament. Although written in Latin, probably in the fourteenth century, by an author unknown to history, *Modus Tenendi Parliamentum* [*Manner of Holding Parliament*] was the first book written on the subject, but it was not translated and published until about 1572. It is a short work dealing with topics such as the Speaker, the Clerks, the Porters, the Cryers, the seats of members, the days, and so forth.[45] The first book to focus on actual rules, written in English, was John Hooker's *The Order and Usage of the Keeping of a Parlement in England*, published in London in 1572. This book gives some details, including the requirements

23

that bills be read three times, that members not misbehave, and that the right to speak be given to the person who rises first. Some scholars, however, argue, "The earliest formal treatment of the Commons' procedure in English was written between 1562 and 1566 by Sir Thomas Smyth, and was published in 1583, six years after the author's death, as part of a larger work, *De Republica Anglorum, The manner of governement or policie of the realme of England.*"[46]

The following lengthy quotation from Smith by way of Redlich reveals much about the early procedure of the House of Commons:

"In like manner in the lower house, the speaker, sitting in a seat or chair for that purpose, somewhat higher that he may see and be seen of them all, hath before him, in a lower seat, his clerk who readeth such bills as be first propounded in the lower house, or be sent down from the lords. For. . . bills be thrice, in three divers days, read and disputed upon, before they come to the question. In the disputing is a marvelous good order used in the lower house. He that standeth up bareheaded is to be understood that he will speak to the bill. If more stand up who that is first judged to arise is first heard; though the one do praise the law, the other dissuade it, yet there is no altercation. For every man speaketh as to the speaker, not as one to another, for that is against the order of the house. It is also taken against the order to name him whom you do confute, or he that spake against the bill or gave this and this reason. And so with perpetual oration, not with altercation he goeth through till he have made an end. He that once hath spoken in a bill, though he be confuted straight, that day may not reply, no though he would change his opinion. So that to one bill in one day one may not in that house speak twice, for else one or two with altercation would spend all the time. The next day he may, but then also but once.

"No reviling or nipping words must be used, for then all the house will cry 'it is against the order'; and if any speak unreverently or seditiously against the prince or the privy council, I have seen them not only interrupted, but it has been moved after to the house, and they have sent them to the Tower. So that in such multitude, and such diversity of minds and opinions, there is the greatest modesty and temperance of speech that can be used. Nevertheless, with much doulce and gentle terms they make their reasons as violent and as vehement on against the other as they may ordinarily, except it

24

be for urgent causes and hasting of time. At the afternoon they keep no parliament. The speaker hath no voice in the house, nor they will not suffer him to speak in any bill to move or dissuade it. But when any bill is read, the speaker's office is, as briefly and plainly as he may, to declare the effect thereof to the house.

"In the upper house they give their assent and dissent each man severally and by himself, first for himself and then for so many as he hath proxy. When the chancellor hath demanded of them whether they will go to the question after the bill hath been thrice read, they saying only *Content* or *Not Content*, without further reasoning or replying, and as the more number doth agree so it is agreed on or dashed.

"In the nether house none of them that is elected, either knight or burgess, can give his voice to another, nor his content or dissent by proxy. The more part of them that be present only maketh the consent or dissent.

"After the bill hath been twice read and then engrossed and eftsoones read and disputed on enough as is thought, the speaker asked if they will go to the question. And if they agree he holdeth the bill up in his hand and saith, 'As many as will have this bill go forward, which is concerning such a matter, say "Yea." Then they which allow the bill cry 'Yea,' and as many as will not say 'No'; as the cry of 'Yea' or 'No' is bigger so the bill is allowed or dashed. If it be a doubt which cry is bigger they divide the house, the speaker saying, 'As many as do allow the bill, go down with the bill; and as many as do not, sit still.' So they divide themselves, and being so divided they are numbered who made the more part, and so the bill doth speed. It chanceth sometime that some part of the bill is allowed, some other part has much controversy and doubt made of it; and it is thought if it were amended it would go forward. Then they choose certain committees of them who have spoken with the bill and against it to amend it and bring it again so amended, as they amongst them shall think meet: and this is before it is ingrossed; yea and sometime after. But the agreement of these committees is no prejudice to the house. For at the last question they will either accept it or dash it, as it shall seem good, notwithstanding that whatsoever the committees have done."[47]

Activity by other authors in writing treatises on parliamentary precedents and practices followed. In 1689, G. Petyt (London) listed as references for his small book, *Lex*

Parliamentaria, thirty-five earlier parliamentary works or sources. [Some scholars contend that the "G.P." who was the author of this book was actually George Phillips, an Irish lawyer, legislator, and judge.] In his book--a pocket manual for the convenience of members of Parliament--Petyt includes entries from the Journals of the House of Commons relating to procedure,"[48] among which are the following:

(1) One topic at a time (1581): "When a Motion has been made, that Matter must receive a Determination by the Question, or be laid aside by the general sense of the House, before another be entertained."

(2) Rotation of recognition (1592): "It was made a Rule, That the Chair-man shall ask the Parties that would speak, on which side they would speak. . . and the Party that speaketh against the last Speaker, is to be heard first."

(3) Requirement of the negative vote (1604): "It is no full Question without the Negative part be put, as well as the Affirmative."

(4) Decorum (1604): "He that digresseth from the Matter to fall upon the Person, ought to be suppressed by the Speaker. . . No reviling or nipping words must be used."

(5) Germaneness of debate (1610): "A Member speaking, and his speech, seeming impertinent, and there being much hissing and spitting, it was conceived for a Rule, that Mr. Speaker may stay impertinent Speeches."

(6) Division of a question (1640): "If a Question upon a Debate contains more Parts than one, and Members seem to be for one Part, and not for the other; it may be moved, that the same may be divided into two, or more Questions: as Dec. 2, 1640, the Debate about the Election of two Knights was divided into two Questions."[49]

Several developments in the procedure of Parliament occurred during the first quarter of the seventeenth century in the House of Commons. "At this period it becomes customary to fix a regular time for the sittings, the time chosen being from 7 or 8 in the morning until mid-day, and the Speaker is forbidden to bring up any business after the latter hour. The quorum of forty members for the competency of the House for business is settled; the adjournment or termination, as the case may be, of every sitting is made independent of the Speaker and placed, as a matter of principle, under the control of the House. Further, instructions are given to the Speaker as to the arrangement of the day's business and his powers against irrelevant or discursive speaking are precisely determined. Express prohibitions are framed against arbitrary debates on the order of business for the day, and also against the carrying on of a debate on more than one subject at a time. The principle is also laid down that the orders of the day are to give the amount which the House is to do, and that this is to be settled by the House itself by means of its orders. And by this time the custom has arisen of making the daily programme known to the House at the beginning of the sitting, after prayers. As a measure of discipline it is ordered that members leaving the House after the first business has been entered upon must pay a fine. The doors of the House are repeatedly locked, and the keys are laid on the table, in order to secure the complete secrecy of the proceedings. The mistrust of the courtier Speaker comes out both in the formulation of the principle that the Chair is not entitled to vote, and in the rule that if the Speaker has any communications to the House he must be brief: he is to make useful communications to the House, says one of these orders, but is not to try to convince it by copious argumentation. The Speaker is expressly forbidden to give the king access to the bills which had been introduced, as he had done on former occasions. We find, too, at this time the establishment of the great parliamentary principle that no subject matter is to be introduced more than once in a session. Again the order of forwarding bills to the Lords is determined... Finally, we should note, as of great importance, the development which took place in the use of committees and the institution of committees of the whole House. . . . The Committee on Privileges, in which all election disputes were discussed, and three grand committees. . . appear as ramparts behind which the House entrenched itself securely against the influence of the Court and Government."[50]

Another important basic rule of procedure, that of the quorum, was established in the House of Commons on January 5, 1640, the number being set at forty, probably because that was the number of counties into which England was divided at the time. The Speaker had complained of "the difficulty of constituting a House, remarking on 'the conduct of Members so unworthy to sit in Parliament that could so run forth for their dinners, or to the playhouses and bowling alleys, leaving business of great weight.'"[51] There seems a likelihood that the quorum rule was adopted for political purposes because of the fear of the Puritan majority that an unexpected vote would occur during a time of poor attendance, but the first recorded demand for a quorum count occurred on April 26, 1729. The quorum of the House of Commons is still forty (about six percent); in the House of Lords, it is also very low, even after a 1999 restructuring.

Freedom of speech in debate was early established as a requirement of the proceedings in Commons, although not without continued opposition from royalty. For instance, "As late as 1593 the Chancellor answered for the Speaker, Sir Edward Coke, when he made the customary request for the privileges of the House by saying, 'Privilege of speech is granted, but you must know what privilege you have; not to speak every one what he listeth or what cometh in his brain, but your privilege is Aye or No.' And at the opening of the parliament of 1601 the Speaker reported an intimation from the Queen through the Lord Keeper 'that this parliament should be short. And therefore she willed that the members of this House should not spend the time in frivolous, vain, and unnecessary motions and arguments.'"[52] Of course, such attempts to suppress debate invariably led to more debate. It is, therefore, not surprising to find in this period much development of parliamentary rules, some new and some refined from the past. It is also in this period that "we find the oldest of the orders and of the formal decisions on points of order, upon which from generation to generation all further parliamentary tradition has been built."[53] The continued attempts of royalty to interfere with debate and the development of political parties at the same time resulted in more and more vehement discussions in the House of Commons, the chambers being the scene of much vocal intensity, but perhaps no confrontation was more dramatic than one not between members of the House but between the Speaker of the House and King Charles I, when the latter entered the House in search of five members whom he wanted to arrest for treason. When he did not see them, he turned to the Speaker and demanded to know where they were, to which the Speaker responded, "I have neither eyes to see, nor tongue to speak, in this place, but as the House is pleased to direct me; whose servant I am here; and humbly beg your Majesty's pardon, that I cannot give any other answer than this, to what your Majesty is pleased to demand of me."[54]

With debate is often found the desire to close debate. Until 1882, there was only one direct approach to closing debate in the House of Commons: use of a device called the previous question. Patience and indirect methods had to suffice as alternatives. The use of the previous question is often misunderstood because its traditional meaning has undergone a thorough historical redefinition; it no longer is what it once was. Clerk Hatsell reports, "On the 25th of May, 1604, is the first instance I have found of putting the previous question."[55] He goes on to note, however, that the common attribution of the motion for the previous question to Sir Henry Vane is in error.[56] The previous question might more accurately be called the preliminary question, at least in its customary traditional usage, as follows: "The traditional rules of the House allowe the interposition, of a formal preliminary motion, viz., 'that that question be not now put.' This is the 'previous question' which may be placed like a barrier in the way of the determination of the question on the original motion. If it is carried the effect upon the original motion is the same as if a motion had been carried for the adjournment of the House. . . .

"If, however, the previous question is not carried, the motion has a further effect. The original question must be put at once, and no further debate or motion for amendment is permissible. The previous question is therefore, it will be seen, a double-edged weapon of opposition. For this reason there are further limitations on its applicability. It may not be moved on a motion relating to the transaction of public business or the meeting of the House, or in any committee or on any amendment."[57] The reader must bear in mind that this is not necessarily the procedure of today's House of Commons, which *does* employ cloture, or motions to close debate.

Other motions, of course, also existed in Parliament. Motions required a second, although there were exceptions, and the rule was often waived out of deference to leaders. Important motions required notice, and they could be introduced at the appropriate time only by the mover designated in the notice. The House of Commons had two uses of the term "division." Division of the question has been granted at various times in the development of the House of Commons, but it has been acknowledged as a *right* in some cases only since 1888. Division of the assembly or House has been much more common. A vote is normally taken by voice, but upon challenge a division is taken. Until recent decades, the challenge had to be by call of two members. In the House of

Commons, a person taking part in a division would go to one of two division parlors adjoining the assembly room. Members would be counted as they return from the lobby into the assembly room. Thus, in effect, such a division amounts to a roll-call vote with a silent roll call. Thus, various modern expressions in parliamentary procedure developed over the centuries under the rules and practices of the House of Commons. Rules against the reading of speeches and against referring to another member by name are among them, and many items in the terminology of the House are still in use, albeit often with altered meanings. Such terms include "point of order," "amendments," "withdrawal," "ballot," "proxy," "incidental," "censure," "disorder," and "special orders," in addition to the terms mentioned elsewhere in this chapter.

Of course, the lessons to be learned from procedure in Parliament are not limited to those of the rules; there are also the uncounted decisions of Speakers--the precedents of centuries. And at the foot of the chair of the Speaker is a large table for the use of the clerks, a table that has found its way into the history of parliamentary procedure by means of the motion to lay on the table (that is, to set aside into the care of the clerks for an unspecified period of time).

The procedure of the House of Commons was extensively revised in 1832, and from that time to this its influence on what is called parliamentary procedure today has been somewhat less than what it was during its first five centuries, but it remains the source of the term "parliamentary procedure." Most of the legislative assemblies, regardless of how little power they possessed, in colonies of Great Britain had formed their procedural habits by 1832. The story of the privatizing of parliamentary procedure, the adapting of legislative procedure to clubs by means of published manuals of rules, will be told in later chapters.

Chapter 4

American Parliamentary Procedure
before 1801

The colonies of Great Britain propagated throughout the New World several legislative assemblies based on the House of Commons. Those colonial gatherings, albeit with less power than the House of Commons and no tradition at all, sought to reproduce in their halls the rules of Commons. Sometimes the rules were copied verbatim, but in other cases they were only imperfectly recalled; in any case, though, the line of descent is clear.

Perhaps the most basic rule, that of the quorum, should first take our attention. Colonial assemblies did have quorum requirements, frequently imposed on them by the government of England, but they also adopted rules providing for adjournment from day to day with a lower quorum. Thus, there were often two quorums, one large and one small. (Furthermore, the United States Constitution provides for three different quorums in both the House of Representatives and the Senate: one to do business, one to adjourn from day to day, and one for choosing the President or Vice President, pursuant to Amendment XII. Many state constitutions have two quorums specified.)

"Some rules regulated procedure. Such was the provision that the speaker could determine a tie by a casting vote. This was not universal. . . . It was necessary, also, to decide how bills were to be read and at what intervals. The chief purpose of such rules was to prevent a bill from being rushed through the house before members opposed to it could have a chance to protest. Usually one day or some other specific period of time had to elapse between readings, except under extraordinary circumstances; and if a bill was rejected it could not be re-introduced in the same session."[58]

Several rules were adopted on the subjects of absence and tardiness, the time of convening daily meetings, the method of convening said meetings (for example, a drum beat, a bell, etc.), and the disciplining of members for violations of the rules.

"Some rules had to do with the speaker, in regard both to the method of choosing him and to the authority with which he was vested. He was frequently given the right to explain a measure, but was forbidden to influence a decision by argument. An important duty usually required of him was that of appointing committees, though his selections were in many cases subject to the approval of the house.

"Numerous regulations were passed, dealing with the formalities to be observed in debating and voting on bills. These included the familiar rules that a debater should stand, with bared head, and address remarks to the speaker, 'reverently' some of them said. In most colonies no one should be allowed to speak more than once to a bill on one reading, unless perhaps by special permission; but in the Bahamas it was possible to speak twice and in Delaware, three times. If more than one person arose to speak at one time, the speaker should determine who had the floor; and in Connecticut anyone who spoke without such recognition should forfeit a shilling. In some colonies votes were taken by yeas and nays, in some by standing or withdrawing, in some by written ballots. Occasionally it was required that the oral vote be recorded, if a member so requested.

"Various other miscellaneous matters were dealt with by rule. Some regulations concerned the care of records. Others had to do with such technicalities as the right of a member to enter his dissent from a vote of the house; or the provision that if the speaker was not present the house should not be considered in session. . . Thus in some colonies it was thought necessary to provide that no member should go into or out of the assembly in advance of the speaker; or depart the house while it was in session or even move out of his place without leave; or 'presume' to pass between the chairman and a member speaking. In Bermuda in 1698, it was voted that no one 'saving the clerk or in a way of clerkship' should use pen, ink, or paper during the sitting of the house. Silence, of course, was enjoined with much variety of phrase. The Virginia burgesses in 1663 forbade members to 'entertain any private discourse,' while business was being transacted. Evidently bad habits were hard to correct, for more than a century later, this same assembly was warning members not to 'talk, walk about or read' during the session. Whispering was forbidden over and over again in various assemblies, and so was interruption of debate. . . . Another favorite regulation denounced the telling of house secrets or delivering its papers to outsiders without permission. . . . Civility of members to each other was enjoined with great variety of detail. Thus, the Pennsylvania house saw to it that no member perverted the sense of another's words; while that of New Hampshire insisted over and over again that whoever should offend a member should be admonished for the first offense and fined for the second. The quaint little assembly in Bermuda in 1620, ruled that 'in speaking against any man's speech, the person spoken against was not to be personally named.' This familiar parliamentary rule against the use of names was adopted in other phraseology in Pennsylvania, Maryland, Virginia, and Georgia. Instead of using names the one debating was expected to refer to another 'by some circumlocution,' as 'the gentleman that spoke last and the like.' But it was necessary to go farther and forbid the use of unparliamentary language. This, of course, was in accordance with English usage. . . .

"One's personal habits were closely supervised. In New Hampshire it was against the rule to appear without a sword. In Maryland it was against the rule to appear with one. . . In the Bahamas, in 1760, no member except the speaker was permitted to wear his hat in the house. In the same colony six years later, the rules included a provision that every member should attend the house 'in a decent dress.' The use of liquor was forbidden, especially in Jamaica and Virginia, the burgesses of the latter colony imposing a fine of one hundred pounds of tobacco on anyone who should be 'disguised with overmuch drink.' Some colonies likewise banned the use of tobacco. Thus, in Virginia, in 1663 a heavy fine was imposed upon anyone who should 'pipe it' in the house; about a century later the assembly in the same colony, thought it necessary to prohibit the chewing of tobacco while the speaker was in the chair. The assembly of South Carolina for some years had a standing rule against the use of snuff; but in 1717 this rule was declared to be 'utterly null and void.'"59

Three departures from the procedure of the House of Commons merit particular attention:

(1) "MAJORITY VOTE IN ELECTIONS was an American innovation, since the English used PLURALITY. This practice was early introduced in the New England Law of Elections and prevailed partially or exclusively throughout the colonies. On the other hand, the use of the YEA and NAY did not originate until the Continental Congress in 1777. This method of voting by roll call showed how each representative voted." [Parliament occasionally used voting by yeas and nays (that is, roll call) as early as April 14, 1696, according to Hatsell.]

(2) "Although the motion TO RECONSIDER was known in Great Britain, it was not employed there. This was because it was the nature of the English not to re-open anything that was settled previously. But in America, this motion which could be made only by a member who voted on the majority side, was most American in its use. . . Also quite American was the idea that amendments should be germane to the main motion for the British claimed that they did not need to be akin."

(3) "Furthermore, in American Assemblies, not only was debate limited, but also it was the American practice to specify by rules what motions should be used and in what order. On the other hand, they often employed the Committee of the Whole House wherein, as in England, discussion was unlimited. The PREVIOUS QUESTION had quite a different connotation in the Colonies. Here it was meant to suppress the question, while in England it was quite the reverse."60

The procedures in various colonies are discussed in Sanford William Peterson's 1983 doctoral dissertation, *The Genesis and Development of Parliamentary Procedure in Colonial America, 1609-1801.*

The rules of the Assembly of Bermuda (admittedly not a colony, but nearby) in 1620 were taken largely from Sir Thomas Smith's book *De Republica Anglorum,* discussed several pages ago. They are only about thirty-five lines, and they include such provisions as standing up, bareheaded, to speak, the first to rise being chosen to speak, rotating speaking, avoiding reviling or nipping words, reading a bill three times, taking the vote by voice, and standing or sitting to verify a voice vote.

The General Assembly of Maryland adopted even shorter rules for its meeting in 1637 and slightly expanded ones for its meeting in 1638.

Rhode Island, where the presiding officer was called the moderator, adopted rules in its General Courte of Election in 1648 and in its General Assembly in 1664 (where it permitted proxy and described absentee voting, by proxy).

Virginia's House of Burgesses adopted five rules shortly before 1660, and five of them deal with misbehavior and fines of the members. In 1663 it adopted rules again, this time eight rules, of which the last one was perhaps the first no-smoking rule in the New World.

Pennsylvania adopted rules in 1682 and 1683, and these rules are the lengthiest of the colonial procedural rules described thus far.

South Carolina adopted fourteen rules in 1692 to govern its House of Assembly.

Georgia adopted thirty-one rules in 1764.

Massachusetts and New York also adopted rules, with New York providing that the oldest member present would become speaker of the assembly.

In summary, then, the colonial legislatures adopted rules that had some similarity to parliamentary rules but also freely declared their independence in adopting others.

As the colonies began to approach nationhood, they sent representatives to Philadelphia for the First Continental Congress, in 1774. The delegates there promptly employed parliamentary rules: within three days of convening "the Continental Congress had (1) examined the credentials of, and certified as delegates, the accredited representatives; (2) completed its own organization by adopting four 'rules of conduct to be observed in debating and determining the questions'; and (3) made progress toward carrying out its purpose to the extent of adopting resolutions for the appointing of committees to study the colonies' rights and to examine statutes affecting their trade and manufactures."[61]

The four rules to which the above passage probably refers can be summarized thus:

(1) That each colony shall have one vote.

(2) That no person shall speak more than twice on the same point, without the permission of the assembly.

(3) That no questions shall be put to vote on the day on which they are proposed and debated if any colony withes to delay the vote to another day.

(4) That the doors shall be kept shut during the time of business and that members shall consider themselves under obligation to keep the proceedings secret until the majority shall direct them to be made public.

On the following day, it was agreed that the presiding officer could adjourn the Congress from day to day when there was no business ready and that he could reconvene them before the time scheduled.

Only a couple of years later, when the United States of America had become a nation, a federal gathering of delegates, since called the Constitutional Convention, sought to draft the supreme governing document of the new country. On May 28, 1787, the following were adopted upon recommendation of a committee as the rules of the convention:

"A House to do business shall consist of the Deputies of not less than seven States; and all questions shall be decided by the greater number of these which shall be fully represented. But a less number than seven may adjourn from day to day.

"Immediately after the President shall have taken the Chair, and the members their seats, the minutes of the preceding day shall be read by the Secretary.

"Every member, rising to speak, shall address the President; and, whilst he shall be speaking, none shall pass between them, or hold discourse with another, or read a book, pamphlet, or paper, printed or manuscript. And of two members rising to speak at the same time, the President shall name him who shall be first heard.

"A member shall not speak oftener than twice, without special leave, upon the same question; and not the second time, before every other who had been silent shall have been heard, if he choose to speak upon the subject.

"A motion, made and seconded, shall be repeated, and, if written, as it shall be when any member shall so require, read aloud, by the Secretary, before it shall be debated; and may be withdrawn at any time before the vote upon it shall have been declared.

"Orders of the day shall be read next after the minutes; and either discussed or postponed, before any other business shall be introduced.

"When a debate shall arise upon a question, no motion, other than to amend the question, to commit it, or to postpone [the debate] shall be received.

"A question which is complicated shall, at the request of any member, be divided, and put separately upon the propositions of which it is compounded.

"The determination of a question, although fully debated, shall be postponed, if the Deputies of any State desires it, until the next day.

"A writing which contains any matter brought on to be considered shall be read once throughout, for information; then by paragraphs, to be debated; and again, with the amendments, if any, made on the second reading; and afterwards the question shall be put upon the whole, amended, or approved in its original form, as the case shall be.

"Committees shall be appointed by ballot; and the members who have the greatest number of ballots, although not a majority of the votes present, shall be the Committee. When two or more members have an equal number of votes, the member standing first on the list, in the order of taking down the ballots, shall be preferred.

"A member may be called to order by any other member, as well as by the President; and may be allowed to explain his conduct, or expressions supposed to be reprehensible. And all questions of order shall be decided by the President, without appeal or debate.

"Upon a question to adjourn, for the day, which may be made at any time, if it be seconded, the question shall be put without [a] debate.

"When the House shall adjourn, every member shall stand in his place until the President pass him."[62]

It should be noted that the extraordinary confidence and power in the president or chairman demonstrated in these rules is explainable by consideration of the fact that George Washington had been elected to that position before the adoption of the rules.

The Constitution devised by the Convention was eventually adopted, and it provided for the adoption of rules of procedure by each house of the Congress. Each house, of course, did so. In the Constitutional Convention, "the only remarkable debate over a procedural matter occurred over the "Yeas and Nays" clause. . . Gouverneur Morris introduced the "Yeas and Nays" clause, but he wanted a vote to be entered in the record at the demand of only one member. Many delegates objected because it gave an individual member of Congress too much power. . . Instead, the Framers agreed on a compromise and set the vote requirement at a one-fifth level. This debate demonstrates the caution the Framers took in dealing with minority rights."[63]

In April of 1789, the House of Representatives adopted a committee's recommendation providing for rules on four topics: "the duties of the Speaker, decorum and debate, bill procedure, and committees of the whole house. On April 13, the House debated and adopted additional rules, as reported by the same committee, a standing Committee on Elections. A resolution relating to joint rules with the Senate was laid on the table. And the next day the House agreed to an additional rule concerning its sergeant at arms: his appointment, symbol of office, and fees."[64] Let us now take a closer look at each of the four rules.

"The duties assigned to the Speaker of the House by the first standing rule were modeled on those of the Speaker of the English House of Commons. He was to preside at sessions of the House, preserve decorum and order, put questions, decide points of order, announce the rules of divisions and teller votes, appoint committees of not more than three members, and vote in all cases of ballot by the House.

"Decorum and debate, motions and balloting, were governed by the second standing rule. No member could speak more than twice to the same question without leave of the House. No member could vote on any question in the result of which he was immediately and particularly interested; or in any other case where he was not present when the question was put. Every member present in the House when a question was put was required to vote for or against it, unless excused. The previous question was to be admitted upon demand of five members, and its form was defined. Committees of more than three members were to be chosen by ballot. Any fifteen members could compel the attendance of absentees.

"According to the third rule, a committee was to be appointed to prepare every bill which should receive three readings. . .

"The fourth rule. . . prescribed the procedure of committees of the whole house in which bills were to be twice read, debated by clauses, and subjected to amendment."[65]

"The standing rules of the House were twice amended during the First Congress: first, on June 9, 1789, by changing the procedure when a division was called for; and, second, on January 12, 1791, by rescinding the rule that no bill amended by the Senate should be committed,"[66] part of the third rule.

"Only one instance is recorded during the first session of an appeal from a decision of the chair that a motion to reconsider the proceedings of the previous day on the congressional salary bill was in order. After debate, the Speaker's ruling was upheld."[67]

Meanwhile, the upper house or Senate was adopting its rules. On April 16, 1789, Senators voted to adopt nineteen rules, which the following paragraphs summarize:

(1) The President takes the chair; a quorum is present; the journal of the preceding day is read and corrected.

(2) No member speaks to another, otherwise interrupts business, or reads while the journal is being read or a member is speaking.

(3) Members who speak shall address the chair and stand in their places.

(4) No member shall speak more than twice in any one debate on the same day without permission.

(5) The first member to rise shall be chosen to speak.

(6) No motion shall be debated until it has received a second.

(7) Motions shall be written if demanded and read by the President before debate.

(8) When a motion is pending, the only other motions permitted are amendments, the previous question, postponing, committing, or adjourning.

(9) If the previous question is moved and seconded, the question shall be "Shall the main question be now put" to vote, and if the vote is negative, the main question shall not then be put.

(10) A member may demand that a motion with separate parts be divided.

(11) When a roll-call vote is ordered by one fifth of the members, each member shall declare his vote without debate, and the roll shall be alphabetical.

(12) At least one day's notice shall be given of a motion for leave to bring in a bill.

(13) Every bill shall have three readings.

(14) No bill shall be amended or committed until it has been read twice.

(15) All committees shall be appointed by ballot, with a plurality deciding.

(16) The President decides question of order without debate but may call for the sense of the Senate; members called to order shall sit down.

(17) If a member is called to order for words spoken, the words shall be taken down in writing.

(18) Blanks shall be voted on with the highest sum first.

(19) No member shall be absent without previous permission.

The rule concerning the use of the previous question (9) is interesting because it imitates the procedure in the House of Commons, but it is different from the twenty-first-century previous question. "In modern parliamentary procedure, approval of this motion brings the chamber of an immediate vote on the underlying bill or amendments; its defeat allows for prolonged debate. However, in the early Senate, a senator who wanted to delay discussion of sensitive and delicate topics would make the motion and hope it would fail. The second presiding officer of the Senate, then Vice President Thomas Jefferson, wrote this archaic interpretation of previous question into his manual of parliamentary procedure for the Senate in 1801. The motion eventually became abused as a dilatory tactic, which caused the Senate to remove it in 1806."[68] (Like the Senate, the House amended its rule on the previous question a few years later, making it a true motion to close debate, as it now is.)

Although the original Senate rules did not describe the procedure for a division, the actual practice was to take a division by having Senators stand in their places and be counted. In Parliament's Houses of Commons, the procedure was for one side to go forth to a lobby and the other side to remain, with a long list of rules to guide the Speaker in deciding which group would go forth, the indolent remaining in the chamber, to the advantage of whichever side remained. (The House of Representatives used the same stand-in-place procedure as the Senate.)

Thus did parliamentary procedure make a trans-Atlantic voyage. The end of the eighteenth century brought with it the end of an era of revolution in government and in the evolution of parliamentary procedure. But the beginning of the nineteenth century was to bring with it the beginning of another era.

Chapter 5

American Parliamentary Procedure, 1801-1875

What is commonly considered the first published parliamentary manual in the United States was the work of Thomas Jefferson, who, as Vice President of the new nation, was presiding officer of its Senate. During that period of service, he found it necessary to compose a more thorough set of rules for that small body than it had previously adopted. He began work on that project, for which he was particularly well-suited by virtue of his previous service in legislative assemblies, including the Continental Congress and the Virginia House of Burgesses (later known as the House of Delegates), his background in law and philosophy, and the unusual blend of inventiveness and efficiency in his mental nature.

Jefferson's first source for his book was George Wythe (1726-1806), in whose office Jefferson had studied law. Wythe had been a member and clerk of the Virginia House of Burgesses, a delegate to the Continental Congress, a member of the Constitutional Convention, and the holder of the first United States professorship of law (at the College of William and Mary).

More than just a supervisor of Jefferson's studies, however, Wythe was an old friend at the time when the Vice President, on January 22, 1797, found it necessary to write to Wythe: "It seems probable that I will be called on to preside over a legislative chamber. It is now so long since I have acted in the legislative line, that I am entirely rusty in Parliamentary rules of practice. I know that they have been more studied and are better known by you than any other man in America, and perhaps any man living. I am in hopes that while inquiring into the subject you made notes of it."[69]

A second source of information for Thomas Jefferson's manual was John Hatsell's *Precedents of Proceedings in the House of Commons.* Hatsell had been Clerk of the House of Commons for several decades and had published a thorough description of its procedure in 1776 (Volume I). A subsequent edition was published in 1785, and a third in 1796. The last edition was published in four volumes in 1818. Hatsell, in turn, had relied heavily on a two-volume *Precedent Book* by Arthur Onslow (1691-1768) as well as the journals of the House of Commons.

A third source was Coke's *Institutes,* a scholarly work by Sir Edward Coke (1552-1634), an English jurist. Coke's *Institutes* was a common reference book for several generations of jurists, and the work is cited repeatedly by Jefferson in his manual.

A fourth source was *Grey's Debates,* a ten-volume collection of debates in the House of Commons from 1667 to1694, compiled by Achitell Grey (d. 1702), a member of Parliament.

A fifth source was the *Journals of all the Parliaments during the Reign of Queen Elizabeth* by Sir Simonds D'Ewes (1602-50), published in 1682.

Jefferson also used a variety of other sources, most or all of them recording precedents or procedures in Parliament. His intention was to collect and digest rules so that they would be accessible yet thorough enough to guide the presiding officer of the young Senate. He attempts to be fully forthcoming in his use of sources, and in his Preface he concedes, "Yet I am far from the presumption of believing, that I may not have mistaken the parliamentary practice in some cases, and especially in those minor forms, which, being practised daily, are supposed known to every body, and therefore have not been committed to writing... But I have begun a sketch, which those who come after me will successively correct and fill up, till a code of rules shall be formed. . . the effects of which may be accuracy in business, economy of time, order, uniformity, and impartiality."[70] Jefferson is correct in assuming that his work, like many other sets of rules previously mentioned in this book, does not list every common custom or routine rule that a group followed.

Thomas Jefferson's book, *A Manual of Parliamentary Practice*, was published on February 27, 1801, and a second edition was published in 1812. The book has fifty-three chapters or sections plus a preface. Most sections consist of just a few paragraphs. The first section, which deals with the importance of adhering to the rules, is the best-known section among parliamentarians, and it is here reproduced in full:

"MR. ONSLOW, the ablest among the Speakers of the House of Commons, used to say, 'it was a maxim he had often heard when he was a young man, from old and experienced members, that nothing tended more to throw power into the hands of Administration and those who acted with the majority of the House of Commons, than a neglect of, or departure from, the rules of proceeding; that these forms, as instituted by our ancestors, operated as a check, and control, on the actions of the majority; and that they were, in many instances, a shelter and protection to the minority, against the attempts of power.' So far the maxim is certainly true, and is founded in good sense, that as it is always in the power of the majority, by their numbers, to stop any improper measures proposed on the part of their opponents, the only weapons by which the minority can defend themselves against similar attempts from those in power, are the forms and rules of proceeding, which have been adopted as they were found necessary from time to time, and are become the law of the House; by a strict adherence to which, the weaker party can only be protected from those irregularities and abuses, which these forms were intended to check, and which the wantonness of power is but too often apt to suggest to large and successful majorities. 2 *Hats.* 171, 172.

"And whether these forms be all cases the most rational or not, is really not of so great importance. It is much more material that there should be a rule to go by, than what that rule is; that there may be a uniformity of proceeding in business, not subject to the caprice of the Speaker, or captiousness of the members. It is very material that order, decency, and regularity be preserved in a dignified public body. 2 *Hats.* 149.

"And in 1698 the Lords say, 'the reasonableness of what is desired is never considered by us, for we are bound to consider nothing but what is usual. Matters of form are essential to government, and 'tis of consequence to be in the right. All the reason for forms is custom, and the law of forms is practice; and reason is quite out of doors. Some particular customs may not be grounded on reason, and no good account can be given of them; and yet many nations are zealous for them; and Englishmen are as zealous as any others to pursue their old forms and methods.' 4 *Hats.* 258."[71]

All or nearly all of the above first section of Jefferson's *Manual* is taken, as Jefferson admits, from Hatsell's *Precedents.*

The quorum is discussed in Section VI, but, once again, the chapter consists entirely or almost entirely of quotations from other sources. Jefferson seldom establishes rules; he compiles them.

In Section IX he writes of the Speaker, not of the United States House of Representatives but of the British House of Commons, comparing him to the presiding officer of the Senate of the United States.

Many sections, such as those on the examination of witnesses, treaties, impeachment, amendments between the House and the Senate, and some others, are of little interest to the modern parliamentarian, but the remaining sections are of more interest.

After the first thirteen sections, the book becomes more relevant to current parliamentarians. Section XIV deals with the order of business in the Senate (five categories in Jefferson's time). Section XVII deals with order in debate and sets forth the usual rules of the time on the subject, including a citation to the effect that no one can speak more than once to the same bill on the same day, although several exceptions are given, and another citation, to the effect that Senators may not disturb speakers by hissing, coughing, or spitting. This section on order in debate is one of the two longest in the book, the other being on privilege. In Section XX, Jefferson writes about motions, including the requirement of a second, reduction of motions to written form, and so forth. Several sections concern the processing of bills. Section XXX deals with quasi-committee of the whole. Section XXXIII gives privileged questions, has some brief lists showing their rank or precedence, and compares the terms used in Parliament to those used in the Senate; Jefferson, incidentally, defines privileged questions much more broadly than modern parliamentarians do. Section XXXIV treats of the motion for the previous question, and the following section treats of amendments, and the one following that treats of division of the question. Later in the book are brief sections on adjournment and on putting questions to a vote as well as a section on journals. There is also a lengthy section on divisions of the house.

Of special interest are Sections XXXVIII and XL. These sections concern co-existing questions and equivalent questions, the latter being unique to a house in a two-house system. In them, Jefferson offers five options when a bill comes from the other house: to agree, to disagree, to recede, to insist, and to adhere. Terminology of this sort does not occur in the Hatsell reference.

The final sections, excepting a section on reconsideration, are of little interest to modern parliamentarians. On the subject of reconsideration of a motion, Jefferson quotes the Senate rule expressly providing for it (if moved by any member of the majority) and gives an instance of it from January, 1798, but he also comments that, in Parliament, reconsideration of an adopted proposal is not in order during the same session. He also notes that what is nowadays called renewal (offering the same motion after a previous version has been rejected) is not permitted in Parliament.

Thus, though Jefferson's book does not claim a high degree of originality and is not the best writing of the great author, it is commonly considered the first published American manual of parliamentary procedure. He had written previously on parliamentary procedure, but not for publication.

For example, during the Continental Congress, Jefferson had put his parliamentary expertise to work in a three-man committee to draft rules for the Congress. The committee presented ten rules, and their numerals and many of the words are in Jefferson's handwriting.

Also, for many years, Jefferson had kept a personal guidebook on parliamentary procedure. Although he never published it, he consulted and added to it often. This set of notes, called his *Parliamentary Pocket-Book,* was eventually bound and placed with his personal papers long after his two terms as President of the United States. This manuscript consists of 588 handwritten paragraphs, of which 286 are procedural and 302 related to constitutional matters. Like his *Manual*, this manuscript, first published in 1988, is largely quotations from English parliamentary writers. The *Pocket-Book* is longer than his *Manual* but is mostly citations of Parliament's rules and precedents.

For decades before writing his 1801 manual, Jefferson had had legislative experience. "In 1769, Jefferson became a member of the [Virginia] House of Burgesses and there practiced parliamentary procedure under the tutelage of three powerful friends: Peyton Randolph, the influential Speaker; George Wythe, the Clerk of the House and its parliamentary advisor; and Edmund Pendleton, the adroit parliamentarian and leader of the conservatives. . . . Jefferson served on this influential [rules] committee and Pendleton was its chairman. The committee's study of the rules of the House--the first general revision in more than a century--immersed Jefferson in what he called the 'minute practices' of parliamentary procedure, and it may have been the occasion for discussions about the intricacies of the previous question."[72]

Over the years after 1801, the rules of both houses of the United States Congress evolved. The Senate considered itself a continuing body from term to term, and therefore it regarded its previous rules as being in effect without further action, and therefore there seemed to be no particular time when revision was logical. There was a major revision in 1828, and there was another in 1877. The Senate was quite conservative in its rule-making and rule-amending. The House rules, in contrast, were modified frequently, with many amendments in 1860 and 1880, for instance.

And in 1861, when several states seceded from the Union and formed the Confederate States of America, they adopted rules in a Provisional Congress for one year and then a Permanent Congress. Just as the Constitution of the Confederacy was based on the United States Constitution, so were the rules of the two houses of the Confederate Congress based on the United States Congressional rules. The Rules Committee of the Provisional Congress formulated twenty-nine rules in one evening of work, which were adopted, with one minor amendment, on February 5, 1861. All but one of the adopted rules show strong parallelism (in many cases, verbatim imitation) with those of the United States House or Senate. Rule 29 established Jefferson's *Manual* as the default parliamentary authority. Rule 24 is the unique outlier: it forbade the use of the motion for the previous question as it was then used in the United States Congress, and it established a new motion, known as just "the question," which, if adopted, closed debate on the *immediately* pending question. The motion for the previous question was, at this time, understood in the United States Congress to result, if adopted, in closing debate on the pending main motion *as well as* on all pending subsidiary motions to amend or commit--and barring any further subsidiary motions except to lay on the table.

But, as with the ancient Greeks and Romans, the procedure of governmental assemblies did not replicate itself in private clubs, and in the United States citizens formed private clubs almost with a fervor--clubs in need of procedural guidance. It was only a few years later that Alexis de Tocqueville (1805-59), French traveler and writer, observed and wrote of this passionate habit of Americans: in his *Democracy in America,* he asserted, "Americans of all ages, all conditions, and all dispositions, constantly form associations. They have not only commercial and manufacturing companies, in which all take part, but associations of a thousand other kinds--religious, moral, futile, general and restricted, enormous or diminutive. The Americans make associations to govern entertainments, to found seminaries, to build inns, to construct churches, to diffuse books, to send missionaries to the antipodes; they found in this manner hospitals, prisons, and schools. If it be proposed to inculcate some truth, or to foster some feeling by the encouragement of a great example, they form a society. Wherever at the head of some new undertaking, you see the government of France, or a man of rank in England, in the United States you will be sure to find an association."

To meet this need, Jefferson's work was not meant to be an adequate guide, but a later work by Luther S. Cushing attempted to be exactly that.

After studying law at Harvard and serving for twelve years as clerk of the Massachusetts House of Representatives, he produced his *Manual of Parliamentary Practice* (Jefferson's title again) in 1844. Cushing, though coming from a legislative background, clearly intended his manual for private associations, assemblies not legislative in their nature. His book is about the same length as Jefferson's *Manual,* and, like the Jefferson work, it is divided into short sections of a few paragraphs each.

Because he omits legislative material and historical citations, Cushing is able to present his procedures in greater detail than Jefferson did. Like Jefferson, however, he begins with rules on the quorum and the presiding officer; afterwards, he devotes much of his work to descriptions of various motions or questions, which he divides into the categories of privileged, incidental, and subsidiary, and other. (Whereas Jefferson considered almost any motion other than a main one to be privileged in that it took priority over the main motion, Cushing allows only three motions to have the particular title of "privileged": adjournments, questions of privilege, and orders of the day.) Cushing then devotes some pages to debate, to reconsideration, and to committees. He then concludes. The rules of debate provide the usual items: rules about standing, with head uncovered, rules about avoiding the use of names of other members, and so forth. They provide for one speech per member per question, although there are exceptions.

Cushing's manual is unlike Jefferson's in certain ways. As mentioned, it was aimed at private associations. Secondly, it seldom refers to specific authorities other than itself. Quotations are rare. It is an original composition, not a compilation. Thirdly, it says it is only part of a future comprehensive work.

The chief weakness of Cushing's manual, however, is what the author perceived to be a strength: the fact that it contains *only* what he takes to be common parliamentary law. It merely describes what the law is; it does not prescribe entirely what should or must be done in an organization. As a result, it provides no advice on certain points and only options from which to choose on other points. He even acknowledges that readers must be mindful that the book does not contain the special rules that legislative assemblies use as their procedural foundation. In a sense, then, the book is incomplete in what it provides for non-legislative assemblies.

Whereas Jefferson used the terms "main question" and "privileged" question as categories of motions, Cushing used "main question," "privileged," "subsidiary," and "incidental."

Cushing also published, in 1856, shortly before his death, a large (over a thousand pages) volume entitled *Elements of the Law and Practice of Legislative Assemblies in the United States of America*, also known as *Lex Parliamentaria Americana*. This monumental work describes procedure in Parliament, in the United States Senate and House, and in the houses of the state legislatures. Although it relies in part on Sir Thomas Erskine May's *Treatise on the Law, Privileges, Proceedings and Usage of Parliament,* it is a masterpiece of efficient research: "To go through 300 volumes must have been a herculean labour. Indeed, the wonder is not that Cushing should have taken twelve more years to complete a work which by 1844 he had for some time been preparing, but that he managed to complete it so soon. That the consultation [of previous parliamentary works] was the reverse of perfunctory is shown by the fact in the second division of Part VI (which deals with order in debate) there are no less than 110 references to 47 of the 83 volumes of the *Parliamentary Register,* and 347 references to 94 of the 144 volumes of Hansard's *Parliamentary Debates.*"[73]

Both of Cushing's books underwent several editions, some of which involved slight revisions by do-gooders who would improve on his work by adding to it their own idiosyncrasies. His manual was revised in 1877 by his brother, Edmund L. Cushing, in 1886 by William L. Allison, in 1887 by Frances P. Sullivan, in 1890 by John Freeman Baker, in 1895 by John James Ingalls, in 1901 by Albert S. Bolles, in 1912 by Charles K. Gaines, and in 1925 by Paul E. Lowe. And in 1964 it was republished under the title *Modern Rules of Order.*

Cushing had a sort of successor in William Robinson, who, like Cushing, had been a clerk in the House of Representatives of Massachusetts. He was also a writer under the pen name of Warrington, and he produced in 1875 a small book (96 pages) under the title *Warrington's Manual,* which he considered a mixture of rules, advice, and principles for legislators and members of private clubs. But the book never acquired much popularity, and the author died in 1876. (An interesting sidelight of Robinson's achievement is that his daughter, Harriette Shattuck, produced a very popular book on procedure a few decades later, entitled *Women's Manual of Parliamentary Law,* as well as two other books on parliamentary procedure. Hers was one of several books aimed at women during the period from 1890 to 1910, when women's interests were growing beyond the traditional domestic ones and they were flocking to form and join associations of charitable, educational, and artistic purposes.)

Chapter 6

American Parliamentary Procedure, 1876-1949

The history of American parliamentary procedure during the period 1876-1949 is largely the history of Henry M. Robert's influence. At the beginning of the period, clubs and other organizations had no practical choice except to rely on Cushing's *Manual* for parliamentary guidance. What was not necessary in that work was the legislative background of the author, the occasional elegancies of style, and the stated assumption that organizations already had a set of rules for which a manual was merely a supplement. What was desirable--and what Cushing's work did not have--was a comprehensive approach and an assertive attitude that would not hesitate to make a complete set of arbitrary but pragmatic rules for all organizations rather than just a description of what was allegedly common parliamentary law.

The author of such a work would have to possess an especially orderly mind, an understanding of function more than a feeling for beauty of style, and sufficient emotional conviction to set forth his beliefs and preferences as *rules of order*. In short, the author would have to be a creator, not just a compiler, as admittedly both Cushing and Jefferson, on the whole, were.

Such an author was to be Henry M. Robert. His military training (he entered West Point in 1853 and graduated four years later with high honor) provided or at least confirmed the orderliness of his mind. His engineering work (he was an assistant professor practical military engineering, constructed the defenses for the city of Washington, D.C., at the outbreak of the Civil War, and later oversaw the construction of the original Galveston Seawall) for the Army Corps of Engineers revealed his ability to emphasize utility or functionalism. His lifelong fervent religious convictions (his father was a Baptist minister, and Robert practiced strong religious beliefs, often taking an active part in church organizations, throughout his own life) paralleled and perhaps accentuated his willingness to enunciate principles for others to follow in determining matters of rightness and wrongness.

Henry Martyn Robert was born on one of the family plantations near Robertsville, South Carolina, on May 2, 1837. "His interest in parliamentary law--as he often related--had been precipitated in 1863 at New Bedford, Massachusetts, where he had been transferred from more strenuous war duty after a recurrence of tropical fever. Without warning, he was asked to preside over a meeting, and did not know how. But he felt that the worst thing he could do would be to decline. 'My embarrassment was supreme,' he wrote. 'I plunged in, trusting to Providence that the assembly would behave itself. But with the plunge went the determination that I would never attend another meeting until I knew something of. . . parliamentary law.'"[74]

A few years later, in San Francisco, then a hodgepodge of people from various parts of the country, Robert became aware of the lack of uniformity of parliamentary procedure in different states and localities. Such diversity only increased the confusion of a meeting, so Robert, desirous of locating a definitive work on parliamentary procedure, inquired into books on the subject, including Cushing's *Manual*, Jefferson's *Manual*, a *Digest of Parliamentary Law* by Oliver Morris Wilson (a 132-page book recently published in Philadelphia), the Rules of the House of Representatives, and whatever else was available.

Studying these works, Robert found not uniformity and clarity but further disparity and obscurity. The number of speeches per member per motion varied. The order of priority or rank of motions was different or unclear from book to book.

Rules regarding amendments and the debatability or undebatability of certain motions were not at all the same. Furthermore, many of the materials that he found tended to be merely descriptive rather than prescriptive and thus were not binding or sufficient to impose order.

Consequently, Robert decided to compose a miniature manual of rules, a fifteen-page pamphlet for himself and his colleagues, to be used in the meetings of the various charitable, social, and civic to which this American joiner and his wife belonged. At his own expense, Robert had the copy printed in 1869 at Headquarters, Military Division of the Pacific. Some excerpts from this pamphlet, one of the great documents in the history of American parliamentary procedure, are given in a hagiography of Robert by Ralph C. Smedley, *The Great Peacemaker*.[75]

In the winter of 1874, stationed in Milwaukee, Robert began work on a manual that would subtract the weaknesses of Cushing and add his own strengths. "Writing such a manual as Robert envisioned would amount to weaving into a single whole a statement of existing parliamentary law and a set of proposed rules of order. His idea was that the book should be written in a form suitable for adoption by any society, without interfering with the organization's right to adopt any special rules it might require. In the manual, rules taken from the practice of the House should be used except in specific cases where analysis showed that some other rule was better for the conditions in an ordinary organization—which did not, for example, have the enormous volume of business to be handled, the sharp division along party lines, or the extended length of congressional sessions with daily meetings. Sometimes the Senate practice might be preferable, such as allowing each member to speak twice to the same question on the same day."[76] In other words, Robert's aim was to reduce from the practice and precedents of legislative assemblies certain rules usable, in a form replete with details and sometimes altered, in every private deliberative assembly. His book was meant to become a set of rules, not to describe rules.

By the end of 1874, Robert had completed his work and had arranged for the printing of four thousand copies, but the limitation of the printer's facilities required that only sixteen pages be printed at a time. Although Burdick and Armitage, Printers, of Milwaukee did the printing, Robert personally selected the typeface and dictated the process of making up and arranging the book, which was a pocket-sized manual. While the slow printing was progressing, Robert's wife suggested that he write some sort of appendix for the benefit of persons inexperienced in meetings. He complied, producing a segment nearly half the length of the larger segment of the manual; entitled "Organization and Conduct of Business," it deals with the formative meetings of an organization, various officers and committees, conventions and mass meeting, the purposes of certain motions, and a few other items. This portion of the book became Part II, and the complete book was 176 pages.

Still, the printing of the book, without a cover, was not the same as the publishing of the book, so Robert set out to find a publisher. Rejected by Appleton and Company of New York, he went to Chicago late in 1875, only to be told by the head of the firm of S. C. Griggs and Company, Publishers, "It is quite useless to accept a book on parliamentary law from an unknown. . . Moreover, what in the world can an army officer know about parliamentary law?"[77] But Robert cajoled, insisted, and even proposed to use one thousand of the copies as promotional copies *and to pay the firm* twelve cents per copy for binding the completed books.

Thus, the company published this first edition with the words *Robert's Rules of Order* on the cover, and the author sent out the thousand copies to legislators, editors, lawyers, and officers of various organizations. He did so in advance of the official date of publication, and, as a result, when the book appeared on February 19, 1876, articles and reviews had appeared already and were continuing to appear in newspapers and journals. The remarks of the writers were so many and so favorable that orders poured into the publisher's office, and-- within three months--all copies were sold.

Robert then added a Part III, "Miscellaneous," dealing briefly with various aspects of disciplining members, including the rights of religious groups and the possibility of compelling attendance by a device known as a call of the house. This new appendix raised the total number of pages to 192, including the index. This expanded version was also published in 1876, the printing being done by Knight & Leonard, Publishers, Chicago, with a larger and more readable type. A few trivial changes were also made in addition to the change involving Part III. (Another printing in 1893 added twenty-six more pages.)

Thousands more were published, and legislators, chairmen, and students of parliamentary law across the country continued to praise the book. Public legislatures and private organizations adopted it. Extensive correspondence with the author developed, and one skeptical reader actually visited the publishing house, demanding to see Robert actually practice the rules in the book. He was sent to a large convention and returned in a few days, disappointed: "I went all the way to Milwaukee to see this man Robert get himself out of a jam. The whole thing went so smoothly that there was just nothing to see."[78]

Robert's book was successful because the time was right (organizations were proliferating tremendously), the promotional activities were effective, and the virtues of the book precisely those mentioned earlier.

For the next several years, Robert had to give priority to his military engineering assignments, but from 1912 to 1915 he was able to devote full-time efforts to a revision of his manual. He almost doubled the material, reorganized extensively, and expanded or clarified various items. The new work, *Robert's Rules of Order Revised,* was published on May 5, 1915, by Scott, Foresman and Company. Like its predecessor, the book was highly successful, running (with very minor changes in later printings) to more than two million copies (about four times the number of copies of the earlier book).

And the reasons for its success were, again, those given above. His very title, *Rules of Order*, establishes at the outset that the book will prescribe procedures for processing business. It will not just describe, list precedents, give choices. Repeatedly, Robert says, in effect, that this *is* the binding rule unless the club has another one. He is never content to say, in any words, that these are the various rules from which one may be chosen. For instance, he establishes *as a rule* a limit of two speeches per member per motion per day. His book is a self-sufficient set of rules, not a supplement to rules of the club. He assumes that is what readers wanted. He writes with lucidity, gives precise formulas to be used by chairman and others, and presents details in an organized manner.

Furthermore, because of Robert's extensive and continuing experience in clubs and other associations, his work is one based on reality as perceived by many people in many organizations, not just a few experts in one legislative chamber. Robert kept close to the experiences with which he was dealing in his books. For example, from March 1 to December 4 of 1870, Robert had fifty-three committee meetings and twenty assembly meetings. He, his wife, and an assistant also answered and preserved correspondence.

In fact, his eldest brother, Joseph Thomas Robert, sought to capitalizing on Henry's success and not only established a correspondence school of parliamentary law (headquartered in Chicago) but also produced a 264-page textbook entitled *Robert's Primer of Parliamentary Law*. The book does not explicitly claim to have the endorsement of Henry M. Robert, but its tendency, especially in the Preface, to imply some inveigled, unspoken approval by Henry seems transparent. The book consists of six very brief introductory sections and twenty-four lessons, nearly all of them on motions that are better explained in Henry's books. The lessons invariably consist of a few numbered bits of information about each topic, followed by a script in which blanks are to be filled and formulas recited. It is, in a word, a model of how *not* to write an appealing, effective, or impressive textbook. It may well have made some money for its author, however, and there was certainly nothing illegal about it.

Curiously enough, Henry M. Robert himself produced a textbook of 248 pages in 1921. *Parliamentary Practice: An Introduction to Parliamentary Law* has twenty-four chapters, of which seventeen concern motions. Many of the chapters end in a review quiz labeled "Practice Work," and some of the chapters are drills in the form of scripts. The last section of the last chapter is entitled "How to Study Parliamentary Law," with various suggestions, depending on the conditions of study. *Robert's Rules Revised* also had a plan for study, including "Lesson Outlines," in its final section. Although *Parliamentary Practice* is better than *Robert's Primer*, it remains an elementary textbook, neither thorough nor innovative, and it has little value as a manual or work of reference. It is seldom used nowadays.

Robert's masterwork, published in 1923, is his 588-page study, *Parliamentary Law*. This book, released only days before his death on May 11, makes thorough and patient presentations on various rules of parliamentary procedure. It gives examples, points out strategies, and offers logical explanations for the rules embodied in his manuals. The first 180 pages of the book (and here it must be noted that this is the only book that Robert had printed in a large format, the pages measuring approximately 21 x 14 cm.) deal with motions. Following are chapters on debate, voting, nominations, elections, boards, committees, and reports. The next chapters concern officers, including the parliamentarian. *Parliamentary Law* is the only book written by Robert himself (rather than his heirs) in which the word "parliamentarian" appears in the index, let alone a chapter heading. The next chapters concern members (including honorary members), resignations, discipline, quorum, and sessions as distinct from meetings.

Part VI, which has four chapters on bylaws and other rules, is one the most valuable in the book, perhaps because it adds so much material to the rather light treatment of these topics in his other works. One chapter gives suggestions to committees on bylaws (Robert always hyphenated the word "by-laws," as was the practice of his time) and includes therein a "General Plan of By-Laws" in which he gives an article-by-article series of advice on the contents of bylaws. He then sets forth eight extremely helpful "Principles of Interpretation of By-Laws and Other Rules," with explanations and examples. He then proceeds to give three complete sets of bylaws: one for a very simple local society, one for a large local society, and one for a state or national society. After analyzing each of the model sets of bylaws, he gives a sample set of standing rules.

Part VII, which contains over one hundred pages of questions and answers from the author's parliamentary law correspondence, likewise constitutes one of the most valuable portions of the book. The question-answer format gives 390 items arranged in a logical group with its own index, answering questions on a variety of topics and giving page references to *Robert's Rules of Order Revised* in many cases. Many of the questions are multi-part questions generating answers that are not entirely clear from his other writings.

The last part of the book contains various charts and lists of motions, eleven pages of forms (many of them no more than mentioned in Robert's other works), and nine pages of definitions. The index is also very thorough and refers the reader to a secondary index for the questions and answers when appropriate.

Robert maintained his correspondence and other interests, including photography, even in his late years, despite cataracts that interfered with his typing. In a letter to a friend, written in 1920, when he had passed his eighty-third birthday, he said, "My friends tell me that they have never seen me looking better. I presume it is due to the physical work of this summer. We bought a house last summer, and have been at work remodeling it for six months, sometimes with nine carpenters, plasterers, masons, plumbers, etc., at work at the same time. As the work has been done by day labor, it has required constant oversight."[79]

His last weeks were spent in a sanitarium in Hornell, New York. Upon his death, funeral services were held at the Baptist Church in Oswego, New York. Robert had been such a commanding, well-known, and religious person that he had often been asked to deliver a sermon or other talk before the Bible study groups, local congregations, and so forth, and the notes of his presentations reveal the same concern with organization, precision, and conviction that is evident if somewhat taken for granted in his manuals of rules, Robert was buried in Arlington National Cemetery.

The key to appreciating Robert's influence does not lie in perceiving that he categorized motions into main, subsidiary, privileged, incidental, and other. It does not lie in realizing that he relied too heavily on the contemporary rules of the House and thus borrowed some short-lived and troublesome devices such as the motion to reconsider and enter on the minutes. It does not lie in his modernization of the motion to order the previous question or his obsession with a two-thirds vote in some cases. All of the above may be seen as contributions of dubious importance.

The key to appreciating Robert's influence lies in a single word: popularizing. He took Jefferson's manual and Cushing's manual and made them popular in an adjusted form in a new book. He popularized by means of charts or tables of motions (perhaps the most favorably received items in his manuals), answering two hundred questions in a few pages. He popularized by means of sensible and authoritative presentations. He popularized by *using* past procedure, not merely citing precedents. He popularized by simplicity of language rather than presumption that the reader knew such terms. He gave answers, not options. He did almost everything that a self-improvement manual or "how to" book is supposed to do. Jefferson had no such desire, and Cushing's book was too academic and in-bred to succeed at doing so.

Perhaps Robert, then, only improved upon the work of Cushing. But if that is so, then one must note that Cushing merely improved upon the work of Jefferson, Jefferson the work of Hatsell, and so forth. Thus history is made.

This chapter begins by observing that the period of time that it covers is largely the story of Henry M. Robert, but there were a few other items during that time that are important parts of the history of parliamentary procedure.

(1) *Hinds' and Cannon's Precedents of the House of Representatives of the United States* is the most exhaustive treatment of legislative procedure ever written in the United States. Asher C. Hinds, Parliamentarian of the House of Representatives, produced several volumes of precedents (with complete presentation of cases) from the history of the House (with some from the history of the Senate as well). His work was supplemented several years later by that of Clarence Cannon, also Parliamentarian of the House. Together, their work runs to eleven very large volumes, including three volumes of index. Their publication was completed in 1936. They are perhaps the best source for interpretations of rules of the House that were the source for some of the rules in the Robert books.

(2) *Mason's Manual of Legislative Procedure*, first printed in 1935, is, in its 1989 version, a 677-page work designed for legislative assemblies and other governmental bodies. Written by Paul Mason, Parliamentarian for the Senate of the State of California, the book is divided into ten parts. The first several parts cover rules regarding debate, motions, quorum, voting, and elections. Part VI deals with legislative and administrative bodies. Part VII deals with the conduct of business. Part VIII deals with relations with the other house and the executive branch. Part IX deals with meetings and sessions, and Part X deals with legislative investigations and public order. Mason only occasionally cites Robert.

(3) In 1890, the Speaker of the House of Representatives, Thomas B. Reed, ordered the clerk to enter on the Journal the names of members who were present but not voting in order to show that a quorum was present. This act was a controversial new practice that, almost a century later, found its way into *Robert's Rules*. Speaker Reed was a very powerful political figure in his time, and a few years after his ruling he wrote a short book entitled *Reed's Parliamentary Rules*.

(4) In 1930, the National Association of Parliamentarians was organized for the study of parliamentary procedure.

Chapter 7

American Parliamentary Procedure, 1950-2006

As Robert's little book grew in popularity, the influence of legislative procedure on common parliamentary procedure waned. Legislative procedure has become a thing apart. Many state legislatures have adopted *Robert's Rules* as their parliamentary authorities or guides, and Jefferson's *Manual* has not proven nearly comprehensive enough to be usable on a day-to-day basis in a contemporary legislative assembly.

The only significant works on legislative procedure in the time period of this chapter are the following:

(1) *Deschler's Procedure: A Summary of the Modern Precedents and Practices of the U.S. House of Representatives* by Lewis Deschler, Parliamentarian of the House, is a work of possible interest to the modern parliamentarian.

(2) *Senate Procedure: Precedents and Practices* by Floyd M. Riddick, Parliamentarian Emeritus of the Senate, is also of possible interest.

The popularity of *Robert's Rules* is still with us. The book is used by more than ninety percent of United States organizations. Countless imitations and simplifications have come and gone, and reprints abound. In 1970, the heirs of General Henry M. Robert, assisted by a lawyer and a teacher, produced *Robert's Rules of Order Newly Revised,* a 594-page work (in dimensions larger than the previous books of rules but still smaller than *Parliamentary Law*) that made no substantial changes in the rules of Robert. It did, however, explain the rules more thoroughly, as if teaching the reader, and used forty-eight additional pages of the ever-popular charts and lists. The sequence of presentation of the rules was more logical than in the past books, and the examples were far more numerous. The index was improved organizationally, and the layout was improved visually. Explanations and details were added, and heresies or misunderstandings in interpreting the rules were put to rest. Put simply, the book worked much of the *Parliamentary Law* material into the format of a rules manual.

The new strength of this Robert's book consists in part in the arrangement of the topics: the motions are treated in a logical order (beginning with the main motion, moving up in the order of precedence), which was not the case in previous versions of his manuals, and other topics are separated from the motions. Furthermore, each motion is examined in steps: first, a brief introduction to the motion, defining it and stating its purpose; then, a list of the standard characters that a chairman must know about a motion in order to process it (for instance, is it debatable?); then, a thorough discussion of the motion; and finally, some examples, showing the form of the motion.

A second part of the strength of the book is its thoroughness, as illustrated by the description above. In his manuals, Robert tended toward terseness of statement; the new book, however, explains in almost tiresome detail and is designed to be read by a student of parliamentary procedure in a step-by-step process, without a teacher or a study guide. Yet it remains a set of rules, not a textbook.

The book has been reprinted about every ten years, the latest version being copyrighted in 2000.

But what happened in 1950, the introductory year of this chapter?

It was a year of revolt against some of the rules of Henry M. Robert. An organizational expert named Alice F. Sturgis produced in that year a book known as the *Sturgis Standard Code of Parliamentary Procedure.* The volume had 268 pages plus twenty-five pages of prefatory material, and it directly challenged many of the rules of Robert.

The primary goal of the author was to focus on legalisms. To that end, she claimed that her manual was in conformity with court decisions, of which she cites several, but the majority of these court decisions were before 1900, decisions in territorial or state courts (often under laws long since repealed), or decisions distorted to apply as the author would have them, when, in fact, they do not apply at all.

Her secondary goal was to produce a manual clear and simple enough for everyone to understand, yet the writing is often unclear and therefore not particularly simple, comprehensible, or measurably better than that of Robert.

As far as motions are concerned, perhaps her greatest contribution was an attempt to return to the idea that a majority could decide anything, a two-thirds vote being unnecessary for most or all motions. Although the rules of legislative bodies had occasionally required a two-thirds vote and although Cushing had acknowledged that fact in one nonbinding paragraph, Robert had elevated the requirement of a two-thirds vote to the level of a rule for several situations. Sturgis justifiably sought a return to the majority.

Another contribution, valued by many innovating parliamentarians, was her willingness to abolish certain motions used throughout Robert's works. For instance, she prohibits the motion to fix the time to which to adjourn (but allows a motion to adjourn to be amended to accomplish the same thing). She abolishes the motion to call for the orders of the day, and she also abolishes the motion to commit to a committee of the whole. She rejects the idea of a motion to postpone indefinitely, and she excludes the motion to object to consideration and the motion to reconsider and enter on the minutes. She also simplifies the motion to reconsider.

Finally, she stresses that an assembly can repeal by implication; Robert required specific repeal of a previously adopted motion that is still in force and conflicts with a new motion.

Sturgis makes dozens of other changes from the rules in the Robert books, but if she intended to break the growing trend of the popularity of Robert or to break the alleged stranglehold of his rules on American organizations, she did not succeed to any large extent, despite her attacks on and allusions to his writings as being inadequate, not lucid, far too complex, or just plain obsolete. Although her work gained some popularity with specific associations, with some women's groups, and with some teachers of courses in parliamentary procedure, it never approached the popularity of the works of Robert, even in its second edition (published in 1966), which was somewhat longer than the first and made some minor changes.

Her manual still exists in a much-modified form, with no court citations. Her book had been preceded by another parliamentary manual with a concern with court decisions: George Demeter, a lawyer, first published his *Manual of Parliamentary Law and Procedure* (note the fourth word of the title) in 1948. Demeter produced a set of rules similar to those of Robert but written in a somewhat different style. (There are about 500 court decisions mentioned in the 1969 edition.)

Another attempt to divert students of parliamentary procedure from adherence to the writings of Henry M. Robert was launched in 1974 with the publication of *Modern Parliamentary Procedure* by Ray E. Keesey of the University of Delaware. This book, which had only 190 pages (many of which are devoted to exercises, a bibliography, and an index), attempts to modernize parliamentary procedure, although the modern rules set forth bore a discomfiting resemblance to the rules of the House of Commons during the Renaissance. Keesey decreased the number of motions (Robert having brought the number to an all-time high of nearly one hundred). He eliminated the requirement of a second. He simplified the order of precedence or rank of motions. He emphasized decision by majority, requiring a two-thirds vote for only three situations. He used terminology (sometimes technically imperfect) that is contemporary. He declined to give much in the way of details on various subjects.

In a question, then, did Keesey do anything truly new and modern, something that had not been done hundreds of years ago, thousands of miles away? Probably not. Like Demeter and Sturgis, he acknowledged an influence on parliamentary procedure by court decisions, although he paid them far less attention than they did.

No matter what these competitors to Robert might have said about him, they all paid him the compliment of imitating his greatest single gimmick for popularization: they all use charts giving basic facts about motions.

The most extreme anti-Robert tendencies occur in a popular book entitled *How to Make Meetings Work* by Michael Doyle and David Straus. This 301-page book, copyrighted

1976, asserts that most meetings have their roots in parliamentary procedure and that meetings generally do not "work" well. The authors assert that parliamentary rules of the kind embodied in the rules manuals of Henry M. Robert are fine for formal debates but are counter-productive in ordinary meetings, where the emphasis should be on building a consensus. They claim that their "interaction method" gives everyone a feeling of greater participation and influence. Somehow, feelings became very important in that era. They recommend using a "facilitator," a "recorder," and a "group memory." The trends embodied in this book are still with us, and they might well be called anti-parliamentary procedure.

A concern with law, especially the expansion of corporate law into meeting procedure, as having a bearing on parliamentary procedure is a concern unique to our time. It has generated two books that merit particular notice.

The first is Howard L. Oleck's *Non-Profit Corporations, Organizations, and Associations*. It discusses legal requirements imposed on nonprofit groups, especially in procedural matters. It is not a manual of parliamentary procedure but an informational book with some parliamentary aspects. In its third edition (1974), this book, written by a professor of law, is a 1,000-page tome with several chapters of interest to parliamentarians. Of particular interest are Chapter 43, "Parliamentary Procedure: Origin and Development," and Chapter 44, "Parliamentary Procedure Becomes Law." (Both of those chapters were contributed to the book by John Waldeck.) Also of interest are several of the chapters in the middle of the book that cover organizational or formative meetings, minutes, bylaws, meetings of directors, voting, and elections.

The second is *Managing Corporate Meetings: A Legal and Procedural Guide*. This 749-page book is by George S. Hills, a distinguished lawyer and graduate of Harvard Law School. The author draws upon his forty years of experience in meetings of businesses and other corporations, explaining in twenty-one heavily footnoted chapters everything to be said about the laws that bear on such meetings. Beginning with the procedure for calling meetings, he progresses through chapters on the quorum, majority and minority, decorum, the chairman, debate, motions, voting, usage and custom, and other aspects of corporate meetings. Much of what he writes would have relevance to if not persuasive force on meetings of unincorporated organizations--that is, groups not officially recognized by the state as legal entities. The author died just a few years after publication of his book.

In 1958, the American Institute of Parliamentarians was organized to undertake the study of parliamentary procedure.

Chapter 8

Contemporary International Parliamentary Procedure

A recent influence on parliamentary procedure has been the development of teleconferencing, which involves having members meet *not* in one place but only over a visual and aural connection. This form of meeting will undoubtedly grow in popularity because it allows members to assemble without traveling, but no manual of parliamentary procedure has established rules for it yet.

Related to teleconferencing is the Internet meeting, which is simply use of an international network of computer connections, now often involving sight and sound as well as text, for a group of people. This form, too, will grow in popularity, but it is still rule-less.

Clearly there is a need for a set of rules, perhaps a chapter on teleconferencing or Internet meeting rules in a comprehensive parliamentary manual, just as electronic voting in public bodies led to the development of supplemental rules in legislative assemblies. Just as science often runs ahead of the law, such innovative meetings are ahead of contemporary parliamentary procedure.

Another influential trend in parliamentary procedure in recent years is what might be called the "legalizing" of various details of parliamentary procedure as practiced within organizations registered with the government. Such incorporated organizations are finding legislators more and more eager to manage the procedures of their organizations by imposing rules in the form of laws. Topics often having restrictive legislation include selection and removal of officers and directors, meetings, voting, records, committees, access to documents, and quorum. In California, recent legislation regarding common interest developments certainly minimized the usefulness of an annual membership meeting by requiring that many votes of the membership be conducted by mail instead; the law even specifies such details as the number of tellers. All of the authors of the most recent edition of *Robert's Rules of Order Newly Revised* other than members of the Robert family are lawyers.

Parliament itself was last seen in these pages in 1832. Its procedure in the eighteenth century was embodied in the work of John Hatsell, and Hatsell was a major influence on Wythe and Jefferson. In turn, Jefferson, the Senate over which he presided and the House (which adopted his *Manual*) were together a major influence on Robert, who privatized parliamentary procedure by adapting legislative procedure very well to private organizations, continues to dominate parliamentary procedure in the United States and, to some extent, other countries.

Today, the influence of the House of Lords is minimal, and the procedure in the House of Commons is not particularly useful to private organizations, but a few interesting points merit attention. The arrangement of the chamber continues its centuries-old formation: a few rows of padded benches on each of the two long sides of a rectangle, with the presiding officer's canopied seat at one end of the middle area. The Clerks sit at one end of a long table projecting down the center aisle. (This table, of course, is the source of the expression "to lay on the table," that is, to entrust to the care of a secretary or clerk a document.)

Because there are 646 members (with seats for only 427), the procedure must be fairly streamlined to prevent small minorities from obstructing business. A quorum is forty.

"Sittings of the House are open to the public, but the House may at any time vote to sit in private, by a vote of a simple majority. (However, this has been done only twice since 1950.) Traditionally, a Member who desired that the House sit privately could shout 'I spy strangers,' and a vote would automatically follow. In the past, when relations between the Commons and the Crown were less than cordial, this device was used whenever the House wanted to keep its debate private. More often, however, this device was used to delay and disrupt proceedings; as a result, it was abolished in 1998. Now, Members seeking that the House sit in private must make a formal motion to that effect."[80]

Such closings of the proceedings to the public are sometimes justifiable. Non-members have sometimes hurled objects from the galleries into the House, objects such as leaflets, manure, and chemicals. Sometimes disruptions have been caused by members themselves, but the most famous disruption was caused by King Charles I, who entered the Commons in 1642 with an armed force, as mentioned in Chapter 3. The intrusion was considered a grave breach of the privilege of Parliament, and the whole event began the tradition that the king may not enter the House.

The procedures of the House are a combination of its Standing Orders and tradition or precedent. There are about 120 Standing Orders, ranging from one sentence to one page in length. Precedents are often found in previous rulings by the Speaker.

No seconds are required, although on some formal occasions the Speaker may call upon a person who could second a motion (Seconds did exist in the House for several centuries.)

During debates, the Speaker identifies and announces the debaters, alternating sides. Leaders are generally given priority if several people arise at once. Speeches must be addressed to the presiding officer; other members may be mentioned only in the third person, and not by name. The Speaker may interrupt a person debating in a repetitive manner or, of course, debating off the subject.

The time of debate is limited usually by informal agreements among the leaders, but the House has other methods. For example, debate may be limited by an "allocation of time" motion, often called a "guillotine" motion. It may also close debate by passing a closure or cloture motion. The motion "That the question be now put" is permissible unless the chair considers it an abuse or an infringement on the rights of the minority.

Amendments are allowable, but the chair shall have the power to select amendments.

71

Votes are normally taken by voice; the verifying method is a division, although the Speaker may reject verification if he believes that the result of the voice vote was very clear. If a division is taken, members are given two minutes and then enter one of two lobbies, where their names are recorded by clerks. By the door are two tellers (who are members of the House) who count the votes as the members return to the assembly hall. Six minutes after the names of the tellers are announced, the lobby doors are locked. The tellers provide the results to the presiding officer, who announces them. If the votes are equal in number, the Speaker has a deciding vote (a "casting" vote). If a member rises during a division to make a point of order, he was, until 1998, required to wear a hat, thus showing that he was not rising to debate. (Collapsible hats were kept nearby for this purpose.)

The Speaker has various duties. "It is the duty of the Speaker to preserve the orderly conduct of debate by repressing disorder when it arises, by refusing to propose the question upon motions and amendments which are irregular, and by calling the attention of the House to bills which are out of order (and securing their withdrawal). He rules on points of order submitted to him by Members on questions either as they arise or in anticipation, but any notice of a question seeking a ruling must be notified to him privately and not placed upon the paper. The opinion of the Speaker cannot be sought in the House about any matter arising or likely to arise in a committee. The Speaker is always ready to advise Members of all parties who consult him privately whether upon any action which they propose to take in the House or upon any questions of order which are likely to arise in its proceedings. Such private rulings of the Speaker generally settle the questions at issue, but they may, if necessary, be supplemented by rulings given from the chair."[81]

Parliamentary procedure in countries other than the United States is often a blend of the procedures of a national legislature and those of Robert.

For example, in Canada, Robert's book is often used or consulted but not always adopted.

Among the competing authorities in Canada is *Bourinot's Rules of Order*, which first appeared in 1894, under the title *A Canadian Manual on the Procedure at Meetings*, written by Sir John George Bourinot, Clerk of the Canadian House of Commons for several years until his death in 1902.

In its second edition, revised by J. Gordon Dubroy, also on the staff of the House of Commons, it consists of only 116 pages, of which fewer than twenty constitute a "Summary of Rules and Usages for Assemblies Generally." Most of the remaining pages are devoted to the rules of Parliament in Canada or to shareholders' meetings, with a few pages devoted to "Proceedings at Public Meetings," including labor organizations. Bourinot makes many interesting comments on motions. He notes that to lay on the table is not used in the Canadian parliament, but he explains its use in ordinary assemblies, based on United States procedure. To postpone to a certain time he considers equivalent to the Parliamentary motion to adjourn the debate. To postpone indefinitely he refers to as being unknown in the House of Commons but explains it anyway. In summary, the book is not meant to be a comprehensive manual but is a sort of summarized adaptation of the rules of Parliament to ordinary assemblies. It is sometimes used as a reference manual by municipal councils.

A third edition was produced by Geoffrey Stanford, and much of the text was carried forward to a fourth edition in 1995.

Another Canadian manual, more widely used, is *Procedures for Meetings and Organizations* by M. Kaye Kerr and Hubert W. King. First published in 1984, it was republished in 1996. In this third edition, which has 291 large pages, it provides an almost comprehensive set of rules consisting of 188 sections and seven appendices.

It is an interesting manual, beginning with comments on group communications and president-focused organizations contrasted with board-centered organizations. It then deals with organizational documents, such as constitutions and bylaws. When it speaks of a "residual parliamentary authority," it shows its assumption that many groups will have rules of their own, and the book is then to be adopted merely to cover other cases, thus being "residual." It then covers a variety of topics, including officers, boards, committees, motions, and professional staff.

In an important chapter (14), it establishes a classification of motions: substantive motions, which are comparable to what Robert would call main motions; procedural motions, including limiting debate, postponing temporarily, referring to a committee, postponing indefinitely, and considering a complex motion clause by clause, among others; regulatory motions, which are chiefly motions about the agenda, reconsidering, or what parliamentarians traditionally call taking from the table; and amendments and subamendments (that is, secondary amendments). Yet, in a later chapter, the writers seem to establish a fifth group, "specific appeals," including a count to confirm a quorum, a point of personal privilege, a recount of a vote, an appeal on a point of order, etc. It can be seen from these classifications that the departures from Robert's thinking is largely in terminology and detail, not in substance.

Most of the seven appendices give samples of documents.

A final Canadian manual is *Wainberg's Society Meetings including Rules of Order*, by J. M. Wainberg, now in its second edition.

The United Nations General Assembly rules merit some attention. The Assembly consists of 191 members (the number can fluctuate as nations are born or die), each having one vote. On important issues a two-thirds vote is required; other motions require a simple majority. It holds its annual session from September to December. The work, typically 150 matters, is assigned to six main committees, which report to the Assembly, which then adopts resolutions. The assembly also deals with the UN budget and its assessment of dues to member nations.

The Security Council investigates and acts on disputes or situations that may cause friction, devising solutions. Unlike the committees and the Assembly, the Security Council alone has the power to make decisions that member states are obligated to execute. The Council has fifteen members: five permanent and ten others elected by the Assembly for two-year terms. Decisions on matters of procedure require approval by at least nine of the fifteen members; decisions on all other matters require nine, including all five permanent members. A nation involved in a dispute may not vote.

The General Assembly, at its first regular session, adopted provisional rules of procedure; at the same session, it established the Committee on Procedures and Organization. At its second session, it adopted, on November 17, 1947, its rules of procedure after receiving the committee's report. In later years, some new rules were added, and some existing rules were amended.

There are now several dozen rules, most of them being a paragraph in length.

The first few rules are about convening the Assembly and about delegations, and rule 31 provides that the Assembly shall elect a president and twenty-one vice presidents, who shall hold office for the session. If a president is unable to continue to serve, a new president is elected; no vice president automatically succeeds.

The secretary-general's duties are described in rule 44.

The most important committee, called the General Committee, consists of the president, all the vice presidents, and the chairmen of the seven Main Committees. This committee makes recommendations about the agenda and its items of business; it may also revise resolutions adopted by the General Assembly, changing their form but not their substance.

Rule 51 establishes the six official languages: Arabic, Chinese, English, French, Russian, and Spanish.

Rule 67 sets the quorum for opening a meeting and permitting debate at one third of the members of the Assembly but sets a second quorum, a majority, for any decision to be taken.

The president calls upon members to speak and rules on any point of order, subject to appeal.

The time of debate is subject to various rules. Limits on the time allowed to each speaker and the number of times he may speak may be set by the Assembly, but before the Assembly does so two representatives may speak in favor of and two against any such limitation. The president may, with the consent of the Assembly, declare the speakers list closed; he may, however, grant the right of reply to any member if a speech delivered after his make this desirable. Debate may be adjourned by adoption of a motion to that effect, but on that motion two representatives may speak in favor and two against. Finally, a representative may move the closure of the debate, whether or not the speakers list has been completed. Permission to speak on such a closure shall be accorded only to two speakers opposing the closure. Then the Assembly votes.

An order of precedence is established for four procedural motions in rule 77. These have precedence in the following order over all other motions: highest in rank, to suspend the meeting; next, to adjourn the meeting; next, to adjourn the debate; lowest, to close the debate.

Generally, main motions and amendments must be in writing, but the president may waive that requirement in some cases.

Rule 79 provides what is called a decision on competence: any motion questioning the legal authority of the Assembly to adopt a proposal shall be put to a vote before the vote is taken on the proposal in question.

Rule 80 states that a motion may be withdrawn by its proposer at any time before voting, provided it has not been amended, but a motion withdrawn by one member may be reintroduced by another.

Rule 81 authorizes reconsideration only with a two-thirds vote of the General Assembly.

Rule 83 is the "important questions" rule: it requires a two-thirds vote for important questions, including recommendations regarding the maintenance of international peace and security, the election of the non-permanent members of the Security Council, the election of the members of the Economic and Social Council, the election of members of the Trusteeship Council, the admission of new members, the suspension of the rights and privileges of membership, expulsions, questions relating to the operation of the trusteeship system, and budgetary questions. A later rule provides that amendments to important questions also require a two-thirds vote.

Rule 86 makes it clear that abstentions are not involved in calculating majorities.

Rule 87 designates the normal method of voting as being by show of hands or standing. Any member may request a roll call. (The roll is called in alphabetical order starting with a name drawn by lot.) The Assembly may also vote by mechanical means.

Rule 88 allows the president to permit members to explain their votes, before or after voting, except when the vote is by ballot, but may limit their time.

Rule 90 provides an interesting way to process amendments: "When two or more amendments are moved to a proposal, the General Assembly shall first vote on the amendment furthest removed in substance from the original proposal and then on the amendment next furthest removed therefore, and so on until all the amendments have been put to vote. Where, however, the adoption of one amendment necessarily implies the rejection of another amendment, the latter amendment shall not be put to vote."

Rule 92 prohibits nominations in elections.

Rule 93 provides that, in elections for one position, after the first ballot, voting shall be restricted to the two candidates receiving the largest number of votes. The next rule applies a similar concept to elections for more than one position.

Rule 95 says that, in matters other than elections, if a vote is a tie, a second vote shall be taken within forty-eight hours; if the result is still a tie, the proposal is considered rejected.

The next several rules apply to committees, and they are largely a repetition of the Assembly rules.

There are then rules on admission of new members and the "organs" of the United Nations, such as the Security Council.

Rule 162 says that italicized headings of the rules shall be disregarded in their interpretation.

Rule 163 provides for amendment of the rules by a majority of the Assembly members present and voting, after a committee has reported on the proposed amendment.

Appendix:

A Synopsis of
Jeremy Bentham's
Essay on Parliamentary Procedure

Most of this book deals with rules that were actually adopted and practiced. This appendix, however, tries to synopsize a set of rules never actually adopted or practiced. The manual in which they were first presented is an essay by Jeremy Bentham (1748-1832), the English philosopher considered the official founder of utilitarianism. His belief in usefulness has the obvious corollary that rightness consists of the greatest good for the greatest number of people. Public deliberations regarding laws must be regulated with such an objective in mind, and Bentham offered some fascinating proposals for such regulations or rules of order.

Bentham, son of an attorney, was a precocious child and entered Oxford at age twelve. On graduating (1763), he studied law for a while but soon abandoned it to become a writer on politics, morals, and institutions. He designed model cities, model schools, model prisons, and codifications of law. Eventually he answered a call by Louis XVI of France for legislative reform by writing an essay (equivalent to a hundred pages of print about this size) on parliamentary procedure as it ought to be. Sent to France in 1789, the work, *An Essay on Political Tactics*, was rejected because it was the product of a foreigner. It was published in London two years later, but it clearly fits the present work only as an appendix.

Though it was based in part on the actual practice of Parliament during a time described in a chapter in this book, it remains a work of theory. His ideas were in part responsible for nineteenth-century reforms in criminal law and the judicial system.

The subtitle of the essay, "Inquiries Concerning the Discipline and Mode of Proceeding Proper to be Observed in Political Assemblies: Principally applied to the Practice of the British Parliament, and to the Constitution and Situation of the National Assembly of France," specifies Bentham's scope, and the entire essay can be found in *The Works of Jeremy Bentham*, published under the superintendence of his executor, John Bowring (Edinburgh: William Tait, 1843), starting on page 299 of the second volume.

Because this appendix is divided into parts corresponding to the sixteen chapters of Bentham's essay and because the numerous quotations can always be found easily in the chapter under discussion, I shall quote without notes identifying the exact page of the source.

Chapter I

The first chapter deals with general considerations, of which the most important is the concept of decision by majority. Bentham readily concedes that unanimity is often impossible: "as it is impossible that there should exist a perfect and constant identity of sentiment in a great assembly of individuals, it is generally the practice to give the same force to the act of the majority as to that of the total number." He explains that his first desire is to obtain the unanimous wish of the group, but his second desire is "the will which most nearly approaches it," the will of "the simple majority." He also notes that there can be no act when the numbers are equal on either side and that the will of absentees cannot be counted, but he qualifies his assertions by saying that the affirmative must equal a certain portion of the assembly in order to be valid.

The first chapter concludes with a lengthy defense of the bicameral system of legislative bodies.

Chapter II

Bentham's second chapter places the law of publicity at the head of a public assembly's regulations. In today's language, this might be called openness. By "publicity," he means chiefly the issuance of accessible documentation or other communication giving the substance of "every motion. . . the speeches or the arguments for and against. . . the issues of each motion. . . the number of the votes on each side. . . the names of the voters. . . [and] reports." He also provides for public observation from galleries.

Chapter III

In this chapter, Bentham begins by describing the building in which an assembly should be housed: "A form nearly circular, seats rising amphitheatrically above each other--the seat of the president so placed that he may see all the assembly--a central space for the secretaries and papers-- contiguous rooms for committees--a gallery for auditors--a separate box for the reports for the public papers; such are the most important points."

Most of the chapter, however, is devoted to a "mechanical apparatus for exhibiting to the eyes of the assembly the motion on which they are deliberating." Bentham proposes a large canvas placard above the president's chair. Hooked letters attached to the canvas would present the motion pending at the time, for reference by speakers and listeners alike. Amendments and other secondary motions would be placed on a nearby placard. He further proposes that the rules of the assembly, reduced into the form of a table, appear on yet another placard.

Chapter IV

Bentham here turns to the advantages of a distinctive dress for the members of the assembly, distinguishing them from observers, and to the placing of the members. He recommends that there be no "predeterminate places," permitting each members of the assembly to sit where he pleases at the time, but he also notes that members of the same political party will tend to congregate in the same area.

He further counsels "to require all the members to speak from a tribune, which being the same for all, relieves the individual from the association of ideas which would connect him with a given party. It must, however, be acknowledged, that this method is not perfectly effectual." He later notes that the presiding officer might permit members to make "short explanations" from their places.

Bentham proceeds to recommend a fixed hour for starting meetings and a fixed hour for ending them, with some exceptions.

The final pages of the chapter are devoted to the matter of members' attendance. His plan is financial: to require that the members deposit a sum of money, such as a salary, at the beginning of a session and that they be permitted to withdraw the money only in light of faithful attendance on their part. With such rules, there should be no need to have a rule for a quorum or a "fixed quota," be believes.

Chapter V

This chapter deals with presiding officers. Bentham begins by recommending that there be one person designated as a permanent presiding officer, entitled "President," not "Speaker," "Chairman," etc. He also indicates that there ought always to be present two persons *capable* of presiding. Furthermore, because the president is both judge and agent, depending on the circumstances, he ought not to be a member, but he ought to be elected by the members by majority in a secret vote.

Chapter VI

Bentham's sixth chapter is, as far as the history of parliamentary procedure is concerned, the most important. He sets forth six articles of rules:

ARTICLE I. An act of the assembly requires a proposal, a vote, and a majority approval.

ARTICLE II. Every proposal for an act must be in writing.

ARTICLE III. Once a proposal is received but before it is disposed of, no other motion shall be made except for three purposes: to amend, the put an end to business without a decision, and to reclaim the execution of some law of order when violated (that is, a point of order).

ARTICLE IV. Debating and voting are separate, and the latter cannot begin until the former is done.

ARTICLE V. In debating, no member, after the author of the motion, shall have the right of speaking before any other, but the competition shall be decided by lot.

ARTICLE VI. Votes, when given openly, shall be given as nearly as possible all together, not one after another.

Regarding his last article, Bentham gives several reasons. He believes that "a fixed order [of speakers] is unfavourable to the growth of that intelligence on which rectitude of decision in great measure depends; to wit, in as far as intelligence is the fruit of industry, excited by emulation." Specifically, he believes that a member whose place in the list of speakers is low will not bestow much thought upon his speech. Bentham's second reason is that a fixed order "tends to waste time by increasing the quantity of useless discourse." Bentham's third reason is that a fixed order maldistributes the talent of the speakers, especially the talent of opposing previous speakers by correcting their errors. He also briefly notes some other reasons.

When reviewing his fifth article, Bentham gives two reasons for having votes given simultaneously: the first is that doing so will save time, especially in a large assembly; the second is that doing so will decrease the undue influence of certain early voters.

Chapter VII

The seventh chapter is a brief one defending the right of legislative assemblies to initiate laws rather than just adopt or reject laws set forth by an executive.

Chapter VIII

Chapter VIII is a brief chapter reviewing the progress of a proposal through an assembly. "Let us trace the formation of a decree," Bentham says. "The work which serves as its foundation is a simple project proposed by an individual; when he presents this project to the assembly according to the prescribed forms, he makes what is called a motion... [Every] posterior motion with regard to it can only have one of two objects--either to *amend* or to *suppress* it. There are, therefore, two kinds of secondary motions:--

> *Emendatory* motions.
> *Suppressive* motions.

"The first includes all those which modify the original motion. . . The second class will include all those which directly or indirectly tend to cause the original motion to be rejected; as by demanding priority in favour of some other motion, or by proposing an adjournment of the question for an indefinite time, &c. . . [There are many steps.] We shall here set them down in chronological order:--

"1. Previous promulgation of motions, projects of laws, and amendments.
"2. Making the motion which exhibits the project.
"3. Occasionally ordering it to be printed and published.
"4. Seconding the motion.
"5. Deliberating upon it.
"6. Putting the question.
"7. Voting summarily.
"8. Declaring the result of the summary voting.
"9. Dividing the assembly--that is, demanding distinct voting.
"10. Collecting the votes regularly.
"11. Declaring the result.
"12. Registering all the proceedings."

Chapter IX

In this chapter, Bentham discusses the promulgation and "withdrawment" of proposals. He has two main points.

The first main point of his assertions here is that proposals should be published in advance of their consideration. Although he allows for exceptions, such as amendments, his recommended minimum for advance notice is three months.

The second main point is that a person who is absent on the day when his proposal is to come before the assembly have his name inscribed in a book entitled "List of the deserters of motions."

Chapter X

Bentham's tenth chapter gives advice on the composition of laws. He advises brevity, simplicity, "pure expression of will," and "complete exhibition of all the clauses which the law ought to contain."

Chapter XI

This chapter is divided into six parts.

The first part deals with seconds and with stating the question. Bentham opposes any rule that requires a second, not objecting to the concept itself but objecting to the fact that the rule is so easily fulfilled, serving little effective purpose. He also insists that a motion be read before any speech is allowed on it, and he recommends that there be a clear rule on ascertaining when a member has ended his speech (in a large assembly, for instance, the person ought to sit down to indicate the end of his remarks).

The second part offers two kinds of debate, one allowing replies and one not. Bentham allows each assembly to decide its own rule on this subject, depending in part on the size of the group, but he maintains that, even when replies are not permitted, the person "who opens the debate, should be allowed to speak last in reply."

The third part reveals Bentham's preference for three debates on every proposed law--that is, three readings of each bill. If undue delay results, he permits suspending the rule, but he also believes that the total time devoted to actual debate will be no greater under three readings than under one. His advantages to having three readings are maturity in the deliberations, opportunity for the public to be heard or experts to be consulted, prevention of eloquence as a suddenly persuasive device, protection of the minority, and opportunity for absent members to appear later in a debate.

The fourth part recommends prohibiting the reading of written speeches.

The fifth part deals with other rules of debate. Most of what Bentham proposes sounds familiar to modern parliamentarians: address the chair, not the assembly; avoid use of names; never impute bad motives; never mention the wishes of the king or the executive power; never quote any "justificatory" piece that has not been presented to the assembly; and do not permit renewal of a motion during the same session or before an interval.

The sixth part tersely enunciates the need in extremely large assemblies to elect certain persons to conduct the debate rather than permit all members to debate. He says the "most simple method" is to elect twenty-four orators.

Chapter XII

Bentham's twelfth chapter deals with amendments, which he divides into those that relate to terms, which he subdivides into suppressive, additive, and substitutive, and those that relate to the connection of ideas, which he subdivides into divisive, unitive, and transpositive. Within the first subdivision, suppressive amendments are to be given priority; within the second subdivision, divisive amendments are to be given priority. If two amendments or more amendments within *one* of the above six kinds are competing, the assembly ought to vote "for rival amendments after the elective manner," what a modern parliamentarian might call filling blanks.

The concluding paragraphs of this chapter deal with what the author calls "insidious amendments." "I call those pretended amendments insidious, which, instead of improving the motion... represent it as ridiculous or absurd, and which cannot be adopted without making the motion fall by means of the amendment itself." He continues by noting, "To propose an amendment, is to declare that one seeks to improve the motion, that it may become worthy of approbation: to propose an amendment which renders the motion ridiculous, is a species of fraud and insult... Besides, these insidious amendments are altogether useless. They cannot pass unless the majority of the assembly be already disposed to reject the motion itself. It is therefore to go round about, in order to reach the end which may be attained by direct means. You only render necessary two operations instead of one."

Chapter XIII

This chapter concerns motions to adjourn, of which Bentham enumerates three. There is indefinite adjournment, or adjournment *sine die* [without day]; there is fixed adjournment, or adjournment *in diem* [into a day]; and there is relative adjournment, or adjournment *post quam* [after which]. The last of these "consists in proposing to adjourn till after a future event: for example, till after the discussion of another motion, or of some bill already upon the order-book--or till after the presentation of a report, which ought to be made by a committee... or a communication from the king, or expected petitions."

Chapter XIV

A very important chapter, the fourteenth chapter treats of voting.

Bentham begins by distinguishing between a "simple" vote, which involves choosing only yes or no, and a "compound" vote, which involves choosing one from several. A simple vote is appropriate for ordinary motions, but a compound vote is appropriate for elections.

He also distinguishes between deciding by choice and deciding by lot or chance, and he distinguishes between summary voting, in which everyone votes at once, with no count being taken, and regular voting, in which an exact count is taken as members vote one by one.

Bentham next divides voting into open and secret, recommending open voting in most cases except elections. He notes that there are two kinds of interest in voting: factitious and natural. Factitious interest occurs when the voter has nothing to gain from his vote UNLESS the vote is known. Natural interest occurs when the voter may gain in consequence of his vote, even if it remains unknown. (Selling one's vote is an example of something that would involve a factitious vote.) Secret voting destroys the influence of factitious interest, but it has no effect on natural interest.

When Bentham writes of summary voting, he prefers taking the vote by a visible sign, rather than by voice, especially in a large assembly: "the sense of sight is a more correct judge than that of hearing. The raised hands, or the persons standing up, are always distinct: voices are more easily mistaken. Are the proportions doubtful?--the operation by standing up and sitting down may be repeated or prolonged without inconvenience: prolonged or repeated exclamations would be equally ridiculous and inconvenient.

"Besides, the voice is a deceptive witness: strength of lungs or party feeling may give to a small number an apparent majority, or least render the result more doubtful, and distinct voting necessary." He also comments that voice voting is contagious--it is like "a sort of *war-cry*."

After the summary vote, a regular vote upon demand for a division meets with Bentham's approval, although he dislikes the method of Parliament in having the division taken by the withdrawal of some or all of the members.

The final point of the chapter is to establish a third choice of vote--neither affirmative nor negative but "neuter."

Such a vote would be given when the legislator is present but undecided. By abstaining, the legislator "may escape observation, or he may excuse himself upon divers grounds. But admit a *neuter* vote in a case in which the public interest is manifest, the voter cannot withdraw himself from censure--it will exhibit either his crime or his inadequacy in as clear a manner as if he had decidedly taken the wrong side."

Chapter XV

This chapter deals with committees. A brief chapter, it has only one point of particular interest: two reasons why a committee of the whole house should be used. The first is that it is "highly proper that bills and motions composed of a series of articles, should undergo two different discussions--first as a whole, and afterwards article by article." The second is that it is desirable that, "upon important subjects there should be two forms of debate: the strict debate, in which each member may speak, but speak only once--and the free debate, in which he has the liberty of replying." Bentham also makes a claim seldom made--but perhaps valid--*against* using committees of the whole: they permit the presiding officer of the assembly to take part in debate even though he should be impartial.

Chapter XVI

The last chapter, another short one, endorses the use of formulas, such as the expressions used in putting questions to a vote. The reasons include saving of words, preventing of variations that may have a concealed object, and minimizing disputes. "Everything unnecessary in such formulas is pernicious," Bentham says, concluding with a very thoughtful observation: "The most sublime thoughts are often expressed by a single word."

Notes

[1] *Oxford Classical Dictionary*, ed. N. G. L. Hammond and H. H. Scullard, 2nd ed. (New York: Oxford Univ. Press, 1970), p. 254.

[2] *Oxford Classical Dictionary*, p. 255.

[3] A. H. J. Greenidge, *A Handbook of Greek Constitutional History* (London: Macmillan, 1986), p. 169.

[4] Alfred Zimmern, *The Greek Commonwealth*, 5th ed. rev. (1931; rpt New York: Oxford Univ. Press, 1961), p. 169.

[5] Joseph F. O'Brien, "The Historical Development of Parliamentary Discussion," *Parliamentary Journal*, 7 (Oct. 1966), 11. This excellent essay is continued in the next two issues: 8 (Jan. 1967) and 8 (Apr. 1967).

[6] Victor Ehrenberg, *The Greek State*, 2nd ed. (London: Methuen, 1969), p. 56.

[7] Greenidge, p. 169.

[8] C. Hignett, *A History of the Athenian Constitution* (London: Oxford Univ. Press, 1952), p. 135.

[9] O'Brien, 7 (Oct. 1966), 10.

[10] O'Brien, 7 (Oct. 1966), 10-11.

[11] Quoted in Chester G. Starr, *The Birth of Athenian Democracy* (New York: Oxford Univ. Press, 1990), p. 51, as reported in David L. Vancil, Ph.D., "The Evolution of Parliamentary Procedure in the Assembly of Ancient Athens," *Parliamentary Journal*, 37 (April 1996), 47.

[12] David L. Vancil, Ph.D. "The Evolution of Parliamentary Procedure in the Assembly of Ancient Athens," *Parliamentary Journal*, 37 (April 1996), 47-49.

[13] Vancil, pp, 49-50.

[14] Ehrenberg, p. 60.

[15] George Willis Botsford and Charles Alexander Robinson, Jr., *Hellenistic History*, rev. Donald Kagan, 5th ed. (London: Macmillan, 1969), p. 80.

[16] G. Gilbert, *Constitutional Antiquities of Sparta and Athens*, trans. Brooks and Nicklin, quoted in John Gilbert Heinberg, "History of the Majority Principle," in Haig A. Bosmajian, ed., *Readings in Parliamentary Procedure* (New York: Harper, 1968), p. 89.

[17] Thucydides, I, 87, quoted in John Gilbert Heinberg, "History of the Majority Principle," in Haig A. Bosmajian, ed., *Readings in Parliamentary Procedure* (New York: Harper, 1968), p. 89.

[18] *Oxford Classical Dictionary*, p. 256.

[19] *Oxford Classical Dictionary*, p. 973.

[20] Robert Luce, *Legislative Procedure* (Boston: Houghton Mifflin, 1922), p.278.

[21] A. H. J. Greenidge, *Roman Public Life* (London: Macmillan, 1901), p. 271.

[22] Greenidge, p. 271.

[23] Frank Frost Abbott, *Roman Political Institutions* (n.p., 1901?), pp. 255-56.

[24] George Willis Botsford, *The Roman Assemblies* (1909; rpt. New York: Cooper Square, 1968), p. 467.

[25] A. M. Wolfson, "The Ballot and Other Forms of Voting in the Italian Communes," *American Historical Review*, 5 (1899), 12.

[26] Wolfson, p. 12.

[27] Wolfson, pp. 14-15.

[28] John Gilbert Heinberg, "History of the Majority Principle," in Haig A. Bosmajian, ed., *Readings in Parliamentary Procedure* (New York: Harper, 1968), p. 92.

[29] Wolfson, pp. 18-19.

[30] George P. Rice, "Parliamentary Procedure in Papal Elections," *Parliamentary Journal*, 21 (Apr. 1980), 14.

[31] Heinberg, p. 93.

[32] Heinberg, p. 94.

[33] François Guizot, *History of the Origin of Representative Government in Europe*, trans. Andrew R. Scoble (London: Bohn's Standard Library, 1861), rpt. in Thomas N. Bisson, ed., *Medieval Representative Institutions* (Hinsdale, IL: The Dryden Press, 1973), p. 14.

[34] Joseph F. O'Brien, "The Historical Development of Parliamentary Discussion," *Parliamentary Journal*, 8 (Jan. 1967), 28-29.

[35] D. Pasquet, *An Essay on the Origins of the House of Commons*, trans. R. G. D. Laffan, ed. Gaillard Lapsley (Cambridge, Engl.: Cambridge Univ. Press, 1925), pp. 2-3.

[36] Gaines Post, "Roman Law and Early Representation in Spain and Italy, 1150-1250," rpt. as "Medieval Representation a Consequence of the Revival of Roman Law" in Thomas N. Bisson, ed., *Medieval Representative Institutions* (Hinsdale, IL: The Dryden Press, 1973), p. 105.

[37] C. P. Ilbert, Preface, Joseph Redlich, *The Procedure of the House of Commons: A Study of its History and Present Form*, trans. A. Ernest Steinthal (London: Archibald Constable, 1908), I, viii.

[38] *An Encyclopaedia of Parliament*, ed. Norman Wilding and Philip Laundy, 3rd ed., rev. (New York: Praeger, 1968), p. 346.

[39] *An Encyclopaedia of Parliament*, p. 692.

[40] Erskine May, *Treatise on the Law, Privileges, Proceedings and Usage of Parliament,* ed. Sir Barnett Cocks, 18th ed. (London: Butterworth, 1971), p. 225.

[41] Trans. A. Ernest Steinthal (London: Archibald Constable, 1908).

[42] "New" [4th] ed. (1818; rpt. South Hackensack, NJ: Rothman Reprints, 1971).

[43] Ed. Sir Barnett Cocks, 18th ed. (London: Butterworth, 1971).

[44] Henry M. Robert, *Robert's Rules of Order Newly Revised* (Glenview, IL: Scott, 1970), p. xxx.

[45] Vernon F. Snow, *Parliament in Elizabethan England* (New Haven: Yale Univ. Press, 1977), p. 50.

[46] Robert, p. xxx.

[47] Quoted in Josef Redlich, *The Procedure of the House of Commons: A Study of its History and Present Form*, trans. A. Ernest Steinthal (London: Archibald Constable, 1908), I, 29-32.

[48] Robert, pp. xxx-xxxi.

[49] This paragraph and the preceding five quoted paragraphs are from Robert, p. xxxi.

[50] Redlich, I, 47-48.

[51] *An Encyclopaedia of Parliament*, pp. 614-15.

[52] Redlich, I, 37.

[53] Redlich, I, 43.

[54] John Hatsell, *Precedents of Proceedings in the House of Commons*, "New" [4th] ed. (1818; rpt. South Hackensack, NJ: Rothman Reprints, 1971), II, 242.

[55] Hatsell, II, 111.

[56] Hatsell, II, 111, note.

[57] Redlich, II, 227.

[58] Mary Patterson Clarke, *Parliamentary Privilege in the American Colonies* (New Haven: Yale Univ. Press, 1943), pp. 175-76.

[59] Clarke, pp. 177-81.

[60] This paragraph and the preceding two quoted paragraphs are from Thais M. Plaisted, "The Source of Colonial Parliamentary Rules," *Parliamentary Journal*, 17 (July 1976), 8.

[61] Henry M. Robert, *Robert's Rules of Order Newly Revised* (Glenview, IL: Scott, 1970), p. xxxiii.

[62] James Madison, *Journal of the Federal Convention*, ed. E. H. Scott, "Special" ed. (Chicago: Scott, 1898), pp. 56-57. The bracketed emendations are from Max Farrand, *The Records of the Federal Convention of 1787*, 1937 rev. ed. (New Haven: Yale Univ. Press, 1937), I, 12, and *Documents Illustrative of the Formation of the Union of the American States* (Washington, DC: Government Printing Office, 1927), p. 112.

[63] William Blake, "The Filibuster, the Constitution, and the Founding Fathers," *Parliamentary Journal*, 44 (April 2003), 45.

[64] George B. Galloway, *History of the House of Representatives*, rev. Sidney Wise, 2nd ed. (New York: Crowell, 1976), p. 10.

[65] Galloway, pp. 10-11.

[66] Galloway, p. 12.

[67] Galloway, p. 12.

[68] William Blake, "The Filibuster, the Constitution, and the Founding Fathers," *Parliamentary Journal*, 44 (April 2003), 49.

[69] Quoted in Giles Wilkinson Gray, "Thomas Jefferson's Interest in Parliamentary Practice," in Haig A. Bosmajian, ed., *Readings in Parliamentary Procedure* (New York: Harper, 1968), p. 58.

[70] Quoted in Gray, p. 58.

[71] Thomas Jefferson, *A Manual of Parliamentary Practice*, 2nd ed., in Wilbur Samuel Howell, ed., *Jefferson's Parliamentary Writings* (Princeton: Princeton Univ. Press, 1988), p. 357.

[72] T. Page Johnson, "Thomas Jefferson. . . and the Previous Question," *National Parliamentarian*, 56 (4th Q., 1995), 34.

[73] L. A. Abraham and Geoffrey Bing, Introduction, Luther Stearns Cushing, *Elements of the Law and Practice of*

Legislative Assemblies in the United States of America (1856; rpt. South Hackensack, NJ: Rothman Reprints, 1971) pp. viii-ix.

[74] Henry M. Robert, *Robert's Rules of Order Newly Revised* (Glenview, IL: Scott, 1970), p. xxxvii.

[75] (Los Angeles: Borden, 1955), pp. 26-28.

[76] Robert, p. xl.

[77] Quoted in Ralph C. Smedley, *The Great Peacemaker* (Los Angeles: Borden, 1955), p. 39.

[78] Quoted in Smedley, p. 46.

[79] Quoted in Smedley, pp. 67-68.

[80] http://en.wikipedia.org/wiki/British_House_of_Commons

[81] May, p. 225.